Life in Kenya in the Olden Days: The Baluyia

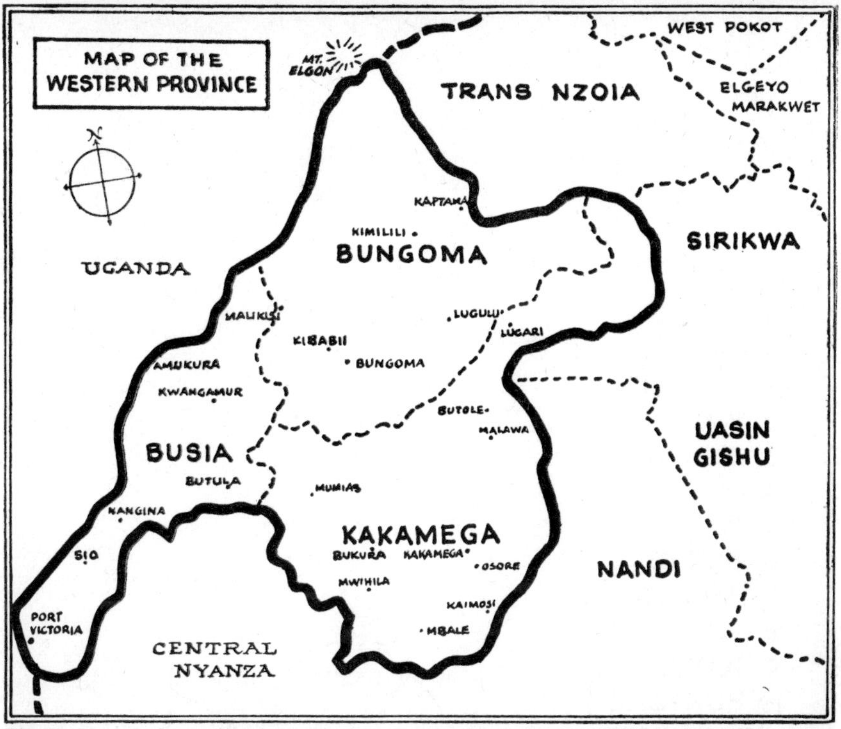
MAP OF THE WESTERN PROVINCE
N
MT. ELGON
TRANS NZOIA
WEST POKOT
ELGEYO MARAKWET
KAPTAMA
KIMILILI
BUNGOMA
SIRIKWA
UGANDA
MALIKISI
LUGULU
LUGARI
KIBABII
BUNGOMA
AMUKURA
KWANGAMUR
BUTOLE
MALAWA
UASIN GISHU
BUSIA
BUTULA
MUMIAS
NANGINA
KAKAMEGA
BUKURA
KAKAMEGA
OSORE
NANDI
SIO
MWIHILA
KAIMOSI
PORT VICTORIA
MBALE
CENTRAL NYANZA

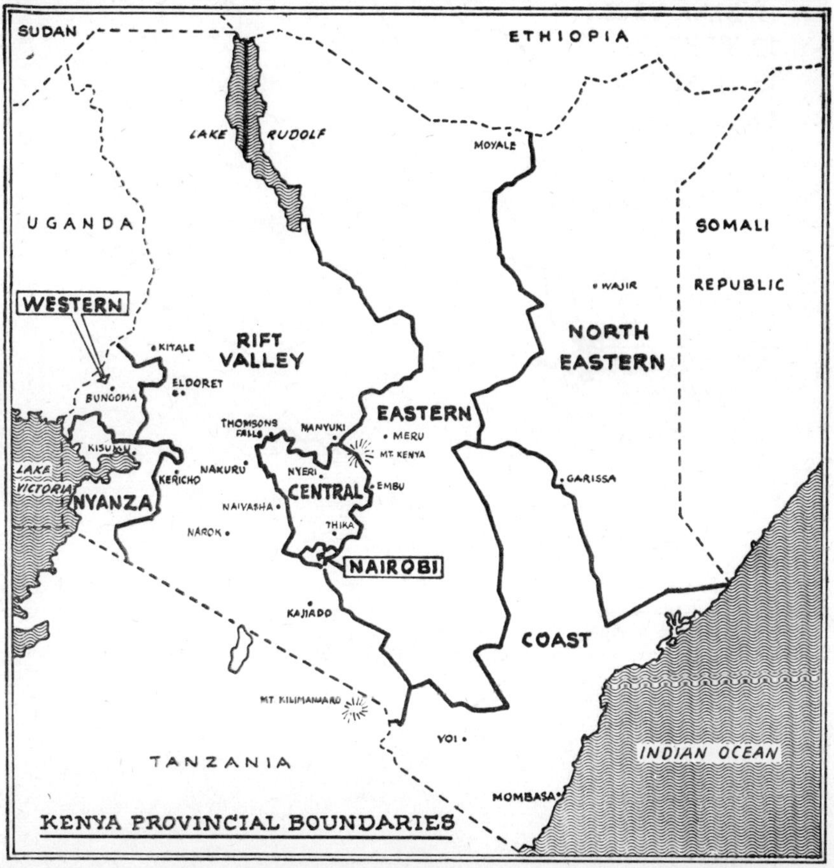
SUDAN
ETHIOPIA
LAKE RUDOLF
MOYALE
UGANDA
SOMALI REPUBLIC
WAJIR
WESTERN
RIFT VALLEY
NORTH EASTERN
KITALE
ELDORET
BUNGOMA
EASTERN
THOMSONS FALLS
NANYUKI
MERU
KISUMU
MT. KENYA
LAKE VICTORIA
NAKURU
KERICHO
NYERI
GARISSA
NYANZA
CENTRAL
EMBU
NAIVASHA
NAROK
THIKA
NAIROBI
KAJIADO
COAST
MT. KILIMANJARO
VOI
TANZANIA
INDIAN OCEAN
MOMBASA
KENYA PROVINCIAL BOUNDARIES

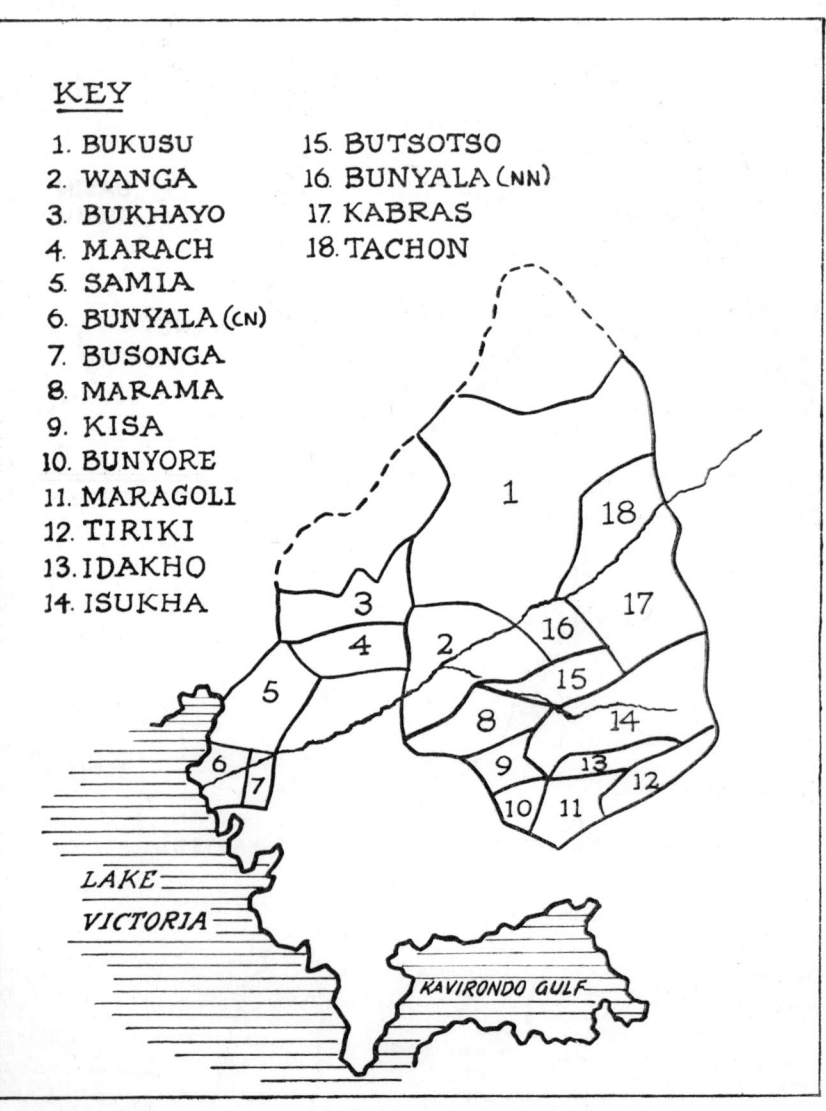

The Sub-Tribes of Buluyia

Life in Kenya in the Olden Days: The Baluyia

JOHN OSOGO

NAIROBI
OXFORD UNIVERSITY PRESS
LONDON   NEW YORK

Oxford University Press, Ely House, London, W. 1.

GLASGOW NEW YORK TORONTO MELBOURNE WELLINGTON
CAPE TOWN SALISBURY IBADAN NAIROBI LUSAKA ADDIS ABABA
BOMBAY CALCUTTA MADRAS KARACHI LAHORE DACCA
KUALA LUMPUR HONG KONG TOKYO

© *Oxford University Press 1965*

Reprinted 1968

Made and printed in East Africa

Contents

CHAPTER		PAGE
	Preface	v
1	Cultural Traditions	1
2	Membership of the Family, Clan and Tribe	9
3	Clothing of Long Ago	22
4	Buying and Selling	25
5	How People told the Time	28
6	Hunting	34
7	Some Famous Founders of Clans in Buluyia	42
8	Great Tribal Leaders of Buluyia	47
9	Some Unusual People	51
10	Stories of Tribal Warfare	54
11	Marriage among the Baluyia	59
12	Tribal Government in Old Times	63
13	Local Government Today	66
14	Shelters of Long Ago	68
15	Obtaining Food and Tools	71
16	Sending Messages	73
17	Some Customs of the Neighbouring Tribes	74
18	The Recent History of Buluyia	76

Preface

This little book is intended to provide information for the history teacher of Standard III in Luyia schools. It is based on the official syllabus, but some rearrangement of the topics covered has been made; it will therefore be necessary for the teacher to pick out where necessary the topics he requires for particular lessons. The section in the syllabus on the method of telling the time nowadays has not been included, but otherwise all sections have been covered in varying detail.

It has not been possible to include here the methods of teaching the subject. This has been left to the training, experience and initiative of the teacher. Whatever methods are used, however, opportunity should be provided for pupils' activities. These include acting, drawing, modelling, writing, examining remains of historical articles, and visiting historical places.

Much of the narrative has been given in the past tense. This should not be taken to imply that all the practices mentioned only happened in the past and no longer take place. The various areas of Buluyia differ in the amount of change that has overtaken them due to the effect of schools, towns and modern ideas. Teachers should point out the customs or practices which are still kept up in the pupils' particular locality.

A selection of clan and tribal leaders as well as unusual people in Buluyia is included in Chapters 8, 9 and 10. Due to shortage of space it has not been possible to select from every sub-tribe. At any rate there are only a few lessons allowed for this topic, and the teacher should either select from those given here, if he finds them useful, or use others from nearer the school area if they are authentic.

I wish to acknowledge the help I received from a number of institutions and individuals while I was planning the writing of this book. My first thanks go to the 1963 principals, history masters (mistresses) and the trainees of the Teacher Training Colleges at Mukumu, Butere, Kaimosi and Eregi, who co-operated so willingly in the collection of most of the material included in Chapter 1. Thanks are also due to the Historical Society of Kakamega Secondary School, and the Baluyia students at Hunters' Trees and Siriba Colleges who forwarded some interesting articles to me through their history tutors.

I am also indebted to Dr. F. F. Indire and Mr. A. K. Hardyman of the Education Department who showed personal interest in this work.

Finally my very sincere thanks go to Mrs. Susan Gores who typed the manuscript so willingly and so competently.

Reference was made to Gunter Wagner's *The Bantu of North Kavirondo*, and Mr. Barker's *A Short History of Nyanza* for some of the material in the last chapter in this book. The rest of the book includes material taken from the author's own book, *A History of the Baluyia*.

Nairobi *John Osogo*
August, 1965

Chapter 1

Cultural Traditions

1. LIFE IN A LUYIA VILLAGE LONG AGO

The Baluyia used to live in small communities. For daily purposes the unit was the village. For other purposes the unit was usually *olukongo*, consisting of several villages. *Olukongo* usually had about five hundred people in it. Some, of course, were more populated than others.

A *village* (*litala*) was often surrounded by a fence of euphorbia trees. In some places of Buluyia where enemy raids were common, the villages were surrounded by a wall of clay and a ditch (*olukoba*) running all round. This made it difficult for the enemies to attack a village, and easy for the inmates to defend themselves. Naturally, walled villages were very large because building the wall and digging the ditch was difficult work and needed many men to work together on it. All the men who co-operated in the work got a space inside the wall to build a hut or huts for their families. Those who did not help were not allowed in it.

The *leader* of each *olukongo*, *the Omwami*, was usually a man of influence. He was expected to make sure that there was sufficient rain for the crops grown on that *olukongo* each year. So very often such a leader was either a rainmaker (*omukimba*) or someone who had influence over another rainmaker.

Activities of each season were started officially, and with a little ceremony, by the chief landowner of the *olukongo*. This was a man recognized by everyone as the heir to the original owners of that part of the land. He started the cultivation, the sowing, the weeding and the harvesting.

Community feeling was very great in each *olukongo*. All the families knew each other, so that a stranger was always noticeable. The people helped each other in most things. If someone had a hut or a granary to build, all the other men came to help; if he could, he made some food and possibly some beer for them. If someone's son or daughter was going to be married, all the others brought fitting presents—usually food—to his or her parents to be used in the celebration. On the death of anyone, all the village came to mourn. The people helped each other n sickness and suffering as well as on happy occasions. This communal feeling is still there to some extent but town life and other developments have made it less binding.

The duties of each person were known and understood. Those of the men and women will be told in a later chapter. Those of the children and young men and women will also be told later; but here we shall see something about how they used their leisure time in play, song and dance as well as other cultural pursuits. Some of these were done only during the day-time because they could not be done at night. Others were only possible in the evening.

2. YOUTH ACTIVITIES DURING THE DAY-TIME

The nature of the activities depended on where the clan lived. For instance, those near a river or a lake included swimming in their daily activities, while those who lived near thickets or forests included trapping birds or small animals among theirs. Some activities were practicable in all places and so they were common.

(i) *Wrestling (Amabwi)*: This was a very common sport. There were local rules for the game. For instance, in the Busia District, it was necessary for the winner to lay his opponent flat on the back before he could be acclaimed the winner. Throwing an opponent down flat on the stomach or in a sitting position or on his knees was not accepted. There were adjudicators to decide and to hear appeals.

In Samia and Bunyala (Busia District) it was further necessary for each contestant to have a fitting rope round his waist so that the opponent could hold it. The Banyala were particularly fond of wrestling. They liked it so much that they held annual wrestling festivals (*amalengo*) which people travelled long distances to attend. The champions of each annual event were greatly respected and honoured throughout the sub-tribe.

For daily sport, wrestling was usually performed on a sandy beach where this was available, or on a flat area covered with short grass.

Wrestling was a boys' and men's game. It still is a popular sport but opportunities for practising it are less common nowadays.

(ii) *African Hockey (Indolo or Obukhuyo)*: This was played with a specially carved stick, much like that used in the European game, at least in shape. The ball was either shaped out of a hard stump of wood, or simply a hard fruit; this latter only lasted for a game.

The participants played in two teams. The number in each team varied from place to place, and sometimes did not matter, provided there were equal numbers on both sides. There were two goals, not necessarily made of upright poles: two stones sometimes sufficed for a goal.

This game was popular with shepherd boys or with adult men. It is not so commonly played today, and only old men know its rules.

(iii) *The Tug-O-War* (*Okhukhwesana omukoye*)*:* A long thick rope was used; and each team consisted of nine people, though this varied depending on the number of people prepared to join, and on local practice. There was an adjudicator standing near the centre of the rope. He started them off and declared the game won when the winning team pulled the other far enough.

(iv) *Olukho:* This was played on a board about three feet long which had two parallel rows of shallow holes on the top side. Each row had eight holes. On either end of the two rows was another, larger hole to be used as a 'store' for the pebbles or special round seeds about the size of a mothball, which were used for the game. There were eighteen holes altogether. Only two players could take part at any one time. The game was played by depositing and arranging the pebbles in the holes, partly according to rule and partly according to personal style. There were six rounds in the game, or as many as would enable one player to win six times. The player who did this, won the game. (Among the Luos the game is called *ajua* and is still a very popular one. The Baluyia of Busia District also call it *ajua*, and still enjoy playing it). Other social pursuits tend to discourage the game in many parts of Buluyia.

(v) *Okhupa Tsinjera: Tsinjera* are special seeds which are oval (shaped like a little bird's egg) and smaller than those used in *olukho*. The game is played on the slightly basin-shaped, four-legged native stool. This is done by holding *injera* between the thumb and the long finger and then by a swift and adroit movement releasing it on to the stool so that it begins to spin round and round on its sharper end. Other players also release theirs and the *tsinjera* are cheered and praised like bulls fighting. The *injera* that hits most of the others off the stool wins.

Naturally, the game was played at home, though during day-time. It was a boys' game. This game (as the *olukho*) requires much time to be enjoyed fully, and so people do not play it much nowadays.

(vi) *Bull Fights:* This was a common sport in the Isukha-Idakho and Maragoli areas. Two bulls were made to fight. People of all ages enjoyed watching this. But it was a cruel game as far as the bulls were concerned.

(vii) *Swinging* (*Mwisubo, Namusuba or Mwirundo*)*:* A rope was tied between branches and young children would swing.

(viii) *Gliding* (*Omuswelero*)*:* Performed on a slippery slope, or using banana trunks.

(ix) *Throwing the Hoop* (*Okhulasa Indika*)*:* Sticks were aimed through a moving hoop.

3. GAMES PLAYED BY YOUNG PEOPLE AFTER SUNSET

These were many and varied from place to place. Only the commonest are mentioned below. Though they were usually performed between supper and bedtime, some of them, especially those for the younger children, could be and were performed during daylight.

(i) *Hide and Seek* (*Umbira Hena*): The children carry one of their number who lies outstretched, facing down. His or her eyes are closed. The children move along singing. The one who is carried sings, '*Umbirahe?*' The group answers '*Ebukwe*'. The one carried sings again, '*Umbirahe?*' and the rest answer '*Embukwe nyanza*'. The song is sung several times in quick succession. When they reach a convenient place they put the one they are carrying on the ground and, using his mother's clan name, they say in chorus: '*Nakhone, salusya amafura khudonge*', which means 'Nakhone, melt your butter so that we may eat it'. They then leave the child lying there while they run to hide where he cannot find them. There are two important rules to the game: one is that the one lying down must be absolutely honest; he or she should keep the eyes closed and remain lying until called. The other rule is that those who are hiding must not go too far; they should hide close by but in such a way that he cannot see them easily. When they are all hidden, one of them then calls the one lying down, who rises and begins searching for them. The more players he finds, the better. When he can no more guess where they are, he announces the fact. Those who are not 'found' then disclose themselves saying, 'I have come out on my own'. They are then declared the cleverest at hiding.

(ii) *Ting'i, Ting'i Teyo* (or *Denga Deyo*): Two children join hands in an arch and the rest, joining hands, pass under the arch in a line singing: '*Ting'i, Ting'i Teyo, teyo, teyo, Khutsye khulire wafwa, Aaa aaaaa omwana wanje wafwa sungila nyokholo* (or *dokhola maseero*)'.

There are local variations to both the game and the song. In some places the song is sung to tease a child who wets his bed.

(iii) *Oliliyo*: The children make a circle holding hands and then walk round at a medium rhythmical pace while singing: '*Oliliyo, liliyo, oliliyo kachenga* (or *kagenda*)' several times. Usually a leader sings the first two '*oliliyo*' while the rest join in with the remaining words. After several rounds the leader brings the song to a climax by singing '*Sing'wandaba*' while they answer '*Kachenga*'; and he adds on, keeping the rhythm, '*Sikhumbari*', while they answer again '*Kachenga*', and so on. During this variation the group dances rhythmically, till the leader goes back to '*oliliyo*' again, when they once more begin walking in the circle.

(iv) *Wangwe Kolongolo:* In this game the children stand in a line each holding the waist of the one before him. The leader of the line (the first in front) is the mother or the father of the children behind her or him, depending on the sex of the leader. Facing the leader is the leopard which tries to take the child at the end of the line, while the mother (father) with open arms tries to stop it. The line must not be broken, but it should move and coil round to make it difficult for the leopard to take the last child.

The leader sings, '*Wangweee*!' and the children answer '*Kolongolo*'; then the leader adds '*Wangwe n'abana*', and the children answer, '*Kolongolo nolie wi kolongolo*'.

Leader: *Wamalira abana.*
Chorus: *Kolongolo.*
Leader: *Wandekhera mulala.*
Chorus: *Kolongolo nolie wi kolongolo.*
and so on.

(v) *Kitumbe ngololiro:* The leader sings and moves round and round, while the rest of the children, joining hands, follow him singing the Bukusu song, '*Kitumbe Ngololilo*'.

(vi) *Ngalabayi:* One child hides something (usually a hard red seed with a black spot called *imbuulu*) in one hand and closes both fists so swiftly that the onlooker can never be sure in which hand it is. Then he asks an onlooker to guess which hand holds the object: he is either to choose *sutse* or *ngalabayi*. If he guesses rightly he wins; if not, the player wins.

It is because of this game that the secret ballot is called *okhukhupa imbuulu* in Luluyia.

(vii) *Gatore (Pick It Up):* This game is played by passing stones. The children sit in a circle. There are sufficient little stones (pebbles) for all except one. The stones are passed round to the rhythm of the song. The hand of each player must pick up the stone on the left side and place it in the space of the player to the right. The rhythm is as the ticking of the seconds of a clock. When properly performed, it is a very interesting game requiring adroitness of the hands. It often happens that a slow player is so awkward that a pile of pebbles gathers before him and he is unable to dispose of them in time. This is the fun of the game.

The song is led by one player while the rest answer:

Leader: *Gatore.*
Chorus: *Gatore.*
Leader: *Gatore.*
Chorus: *Gatore.*
Leader: *Khagina khetsa wekholerere gatore.*

Chorus: *Gatore.*
and so on.

This is a very old song. It is known to be in the dialect which the early Baluyia spoke, especially those living in Ibanda and other places near Lake Victoria. The children of those days loved the game.

(viii) *The 'Linani' (Maneater):* This game can only be played in the dark. One of the players places 'torches' (sticks or thick strings with fire at the end) on his ears, in the hands, between the toes, and at every convenient place of his body. He looks very frightening in the dark and the others run away in terror as he approaches.

(ix) *Aramuchikicha:* The children clap hands in patterns while singing the song '*Aramuchikicha*'.

4. THE SONGS

The Baluyia had many songs for people of all ages and both sexes, and for all occasions.

There were songs for young people of both sexes; others for girls only, yet others for boys only. There were songs for women and others for men.

The songs can further be subdivided to fit the occasion. For instance, there were special songs for weddings—to be sung before, during and after the wedding. There were funeral songs, circumcision songs, and songs for the birth of twins.

There were special songs for beer parties, as well as for the special dancing festival called *omwimo*—separate ones for men and for women.

The songs differed slightly from place to place, both in words and music, and so it would serve no good purpose to write them here. What individual schools should do is to learn the various types of songs sung in their particular areas. Later, when they reach the chapters dealing with, say, marriage, they should sing the appropriate songs again, and so on. When it is possible to record the various songs on tape and pass them round in schools, it will then be possible to learn versions of the songs sung in other parts of Buluyia, for there are many similarities. It should be noted that Luyia songs sound best in one voice—harmony makes them sound foreign.

5. THE MUSICAL INSTRUMENTS

These are many and varied. There is the drum, both the large one (*ing'oma*) and the small one (*ishukuti*). The latter still is a favourite in many parts of Buluyia for the lively dance it makes possible. There is the harp (*obukhana*), the flute, and a kind of lyre (*eshiriri);* there is the *litungu* which is second only to *ishukuti* in popularity. Then we have, of course, the horn, and also the *indongooli*. There are other varieties of local musical instruments as well.

6. PROVERBS

The Baluyia had many wise sayings to teach the young people wisdom. There were hundreds of them. Only a very few are selected here for illustration. The teacher and his class will be able to add many more.

(i) *Olwikho luli munda:* your real friend or relative is one who gives you food when you need it.

(ii) *Oukhumechera akhwaya khumoni:* anyone who gives food to you as a favour gets a chance to control you.

(iii) *Amatsai karula khusalache:* you cannot have blood without a cut, which means there is usually some truth in a rumour.

(iv) *Opilu yibula opilu:* a bad tree bears bad fruit and *vice versa*.

(v) *Omulongi aliiranga khuluchio:* the potter eats from a broken pot, meaning one who has plenty of anything does not value it much. (Also, an apparently rich person may lack quite a number of other good things.)

(vi) *Amadere kabiri kera inda:* two thumbnails can kill a louse, meaning unity is strength.

(vii) *Bira eyale mana wule:* rather take a longer route and arrive safely; or hurry, hurry has no blessing.

(viii) *Nziyukhane yayia ameno:* similar to number (vii)

(ix) *Olia eshititi orafwimba inda:* it is no use eating too much if it is going to cause you stomach-ache; this means rather be poor and happy than rich and miserable.

(x) *Outeeba omurwe niye owakuchinga:* he who keeps wondering who will carry the head of the dead cow is the one who will carry it. This means: what you are most anxious to avoid is often what happens to you.

(xi) *Mama samba esiachi:* when a child has eaten enough, he forgets that he will need to eat again and advises the mother to burn the granary. When everything is going well, we become too complacent.

(xii) *Linda bunyire yalia nabacheni:* if you wait for your food to cool first you will eat it with visitors; this is the opposite of numbers (vii) and (viii).

(xiii) *Ochenda kahala yola e Bunyolo* (or *Mumbo*): go slowly and you will reach the distant Luo country, means slow but sure wins the race.

(xiv) *Khotsanyene abanji yakona inzala:* a person depending on too many relatives often misses food because each of them expects the other to provide the food.

(xv) *Tsimbeba nyingi sitsiyira obwina:* too many rats can't dig a hole, which means too many people trying to do one thing will spoil it.

(xvi) *Khayundiyundi shikhacherera lisoko:* a small bird cannot advise a bigger one. An expert knows best.

(xvii) *Ifulu yacherera ingeke:* the small fish can sometimes advise the bigger one. Even if you are big and important, you can still be advised. This is the opposite of the proverb preceding it.

(xviii) *Eshirukha syenyene shyelayanga tsimbiro:* a person running alone thinks he is the fastest runner. Your real test is when you are among equals or experts.

(xix) *Omusala murerere kunina owakumanya:* a difficult person requires tact. (Literally: a slippery tree requires one who knows all about it to climb it.)

(xx) *Omusyani wa lebe n'okhulya:* a healthy young man who is admired gets that way by eating good food.

(xxi) *Oratseshera akharo khali ebusiba:* don't laugh at a distant boat being tossed by the waves: your relative might be in it.

(xxii) *Ing'u yeweng'u yikhulia yakhulekherera:* literally, the hyena from nearer home will eat and leave at least a part of you; meaning, it is better to accept the evil you understand than the good which you do not. It also means a relative is more useful to you than a mere acquaintance.

(xxiii) *Olumuli lulala silukwisya ifula munzu:* literally, one grass from the roof does not let in the rain. This means no one is too important in any place, for his absence will make no difference.

(xxiv) *Niwenya eshitahalira wira yiyo:* literally, if you want the best part of the cow (e.g. its liver) kill your own. Don't claim what you are not entitled to.

(xxv) *Ikhabi yikwitsanga khuyindi:* success attracts success.

7. STORIES OF TRIBAL BEGINNINGS

The Baluyia say they came from Egypt. They say they descend from Wele —who is either God or our first ancestor. Wele created or bore a boy, Mwambu, and a girl, Seera. (Some Baluyia say it was Akuru, the boy, and Muka, the girl.) The boy and the girl married and bore another boy, Mugoma, and a girl, Malaba. These two married and gave birth to all the Bantu peoples.

Then the Baluyia moved southwards through Bunyoro in Uganda to our home today.

Chapter 2

Membership of the Family, Clan and Tribe

1. THE AGE-GROUPS

An age-group is usually called *likhula*. In some places it is called *oluse* and in others *olubaka*.

People of the same *likhula* are usually born in the same year. In former days, they were, naturally, initiated together; that is, they were circumcised together, and where there was no circumcision practice, they had their teeth taken out from the lower jaw (six or four, depending on custom) together. They grew up together, doing the same type of things, looking after goats, then cattle; playing the same games, and, later, taking part in war. We shall learn something about their activities in later lessons.

The following table shows the terms used for the main different ages.

Age	*Male*	*Female*
Babies	Abatoro (tsindana)	Abatoro (tsindana)
Young Children	Abayere	Abayere
Older Children	Abahya	Abahya
Early Youth	Abasyani (abayayi)	Abakhana
Later Youth	Abasoliri	Abakhana
	uncircumcised: Abasinde	
	circumcised: Abashebe, etc.	
At Marriage	Balikahe (or other local names)	Bakubuyu (obingo)
Middle Age	Batukhu (or other local names)	Batukhu, etc.
Old Age	Abakofu or Abasakhulu	Bashyere
Respected Old Age	Bakhulundu	
	Abami	Abakhaye
	Abenengo	

2. CHILDHOOD

The following were the main ages during babyhood.

Indana (or *olwesi*): from birth to two months.
Libiechera (*omwana otsekhera tsisiye*): beginning to smile.
Omwana ofumbwa: beginning to sit.

Some of these names vary in different places of Buluyia. There are also names for a child beginning to crawl, to stand, to walk, or to talk; also for when the first teeth appear and when they fall out.

An important age is when the child is said to be 'able to fetch fire'. This is generally from three-and-a-half years to five years.

Children of this age, of course, had no duties to perform. They spent most of their time playing. Some of the games they played have already been learnt.

Older children (*abayere*) could help their mothers with little duties in the house, especially in connection with cooking.

Boys older than seven could look after sheep. And girls of that age could help their mothers with more difficult tasks such as fetching water and firewood, or grinding corn.

3. YOUTH

Young people were expected to be happy. Hence there were frequent occasions for dances. Marriage festivals, funeral parties, initiation ceremonies, and similar occasions came in useful for this purpose.

They were also expected to perform certain duties. Boys had separate duties from girls.

(i) *Boys:* The boys usually looked after cattle. In the evenings they kept the 'court-yard' fire burning. It was at this fire that the old men gave instructions to the boys in the important practices and affairs of their clan or tribe.

More instructions were, of course, given during the time of initiation, especially where circumcision was in practice.

Boys who were over eighteen were also expected to join in the regular hunts, and to go to battle if there was a war. In addition, they were charged with the duty of protecting the home. This is one of the reasons why men married many wives; they hoped to get many sons who were to protect the home against attackers. Those who needed special protection were children and women.

In return for the duties they performed, the young men had certain privileges in the home, in the village, and in the clan. During a hunt they got a share of the meat killed. They also got their share of the meat killed for a wedding. They got help from relatives towards the payment of bride price, especially for their first bride.

When building their first hut, *isimba*, they got help from fellow villagers of their age. They also got a full right to join in the social activities of young people; for instance, dancing festivals.

(ii) *Girls:* The girls helped their mothers in most of their work in the home and in the field. In some areas they were expected to keep the *ts-isimba* of their brothers and male cousins clean, by sweeping or smearing. In addition, they looked after the guests who came in the home, especially unmarried ones.

In return for these and other duties, the girls enjoyed full protection against attackers. Their brothers and cousins would fight any other young men who wanted to harm them. Even where a young man had paid the bride price for a girl, he had no right to drag the girl away; and if he did so, the young men of the girl's side would fight back and, where possible, release the girl.

After marriage a girl had the right to come home to fetch certain presents for her husband, or just to stay for a time. Many of these customs are still practised today.

4. OLD AGE

We can divide old age into two groups: middle age and the proper old age.

(i) *Middle Age:* The men(*abasatsa*) had the duty of defending the tribe in a war. Their day-to-day work included clearing the bush for cultivation, building houses, building traps for catching animals, birds or fish, and hunting. In places where it was necessary to build walled villages (*tsingoba*), it was the *abasatsa* who did the job.

The privileges the man received included mutual help from other members of the village or clan, a right to join in the beer parties for social occasions, and a right to get his proper share of the meat, whether from hunting or a wedding or other ceremony. He also enjoyed his proper place in the clan.

The women's duties included and still include cultivation, sowing, weeding and harvesting, as well as looking after the children and doing the housework.

Their privileges still include the right to own a hut and a granary, to get a share of the meat or fish from the husband, and the right to protection.

(ii) *Old Age:* This normally meant people who were over fifty years of age. The old men were usually useful in the house for telling the young men secrets and stories of their clan or tribe. They recounted the great deeds of the heroes and gave advice to younger people. It was also their duty to settle difficult cases, especially those involving ownership of the land, and traditional customs.

The old women were useful in a similar manner, but they were usually concerned with advising women and girls, and telling tribal legends.

Some old men and old women were famous medicine-men; some old men could also be rainmakers; they performed these tasks and were paid for them in cattle, ornaments or hoes.

In return for their various tasks, the old people received respect and kind treatment, a place to sleep, food, firewood and water, a share of the meat, and, finally, a decent burial.

5. THE FAMILY

The family consisted of father and mother and the children. The father usually looked after the whole home. The mother was in charge of the house.

(i) Of the children, the first (*omwana wa mberi*) and the last (*makhokoro* or *walaka*) had special privileges. The first always got his share of whatever was divided, first. He married first and was the first one to leave his father's home in order to pitch his own home elsewhere. Normally he inherited from his father, but this was not always the case. A male child usually had precedence over his sisters including those older than him.

The last child was the favourite of his parents; and, if a boy, was sometimes given the inheritance. In most areas in Buluyia it was the last-born boy to remain in his father's home after all the others had left and pitched their own homes.

Because men sometimes married several women, a home often had many step-brothers and step-sisters and other relatives.

(ii) Below is a list of the main terms used in describing relatives. There are slight differences in different places, but most of them are used everywhere in Buluyia.

Name of relative	Father's side	Mother's side
Aunt	Senje (senge)	Mama
Uncle	Papa (baba)	Khotsa
Cousin	Omwana wefu (-weru)	Mufyala
Cross-cousins	Ikhasi (-yanje)	Ikhasi (-yanje)
Grandmother	Kukhu	Kukhu
Grandfather	Kuka	Kuka
Great-Uncle	Kuka	Kuka
Great-Aunt	Kukhu	Kukhu
Grandsons	Abetsukhulu	Abetsukhulu
Great-Grandsons	Nambunda	Nambunda
Great-Great Grandsons	Bisoni	Bisoni
Great-Great-Great Grandsons	Sisindikisya Mabuyu	Sisindikisya Mabuyu

Membership of the Family, Clan and Tribe

	Brother's side	Sister's side
Niece	Omusenjetsana (by man's sister) Omwana wanje (by man's brother)	Omwiwa (by woman's brother) Omwana wanje (by woman's sister)
Nephew	Omusenjetsana (by sister) Omwana wanje (by brother)	Omwiwa (by brother) Omwana wanje (by sister)

All cousins at all levels called each other *omwana wefu*. That is, even if a family dates back five hundred years, each generation will have persons who call one another *omwana wefu*, just as if they were their own brothers or sisters. This also applies to certain degrees of aunts, uncles, nieces and nephews.

6. ALLOCATION OF WORK IN THE FAMILY

This has been dealt with in sections 2-4; so first refer back to these lessons to revise the duties of the various ages of people.

Here it is sufficient to give a list of some of the most important of these duties.

Men	*Women*
Building houses	Cooking
Getting meat or fish	Getting green vegetables
Clearing bush	Cultivation
Hunting	Looking after children
Going to war	Sowing, weeding, harvesting
Blacksmithing	Fetching firewood
Making tools	Fetching water
Making granaries	Washing
Circumcising	Storing food
Slaughtering animals	Sweeping
Preparing animal skins	Smearing floors
Settling cases	Shaving
Burying the dead	Making beer

The children used to help—boys helped their fathers, and girls their mothers. Older boys looked after cattle, sheep and goats.

Both men and women could be medicine-men. Also, both could clean the cattle boma. In some eastern parts of Buluyia women could build huts. This was impossible in western Buluyia.

7. FURNITURE, UTENSILS AND TOOLS

(i) A Luyia house did not consist of much furniture. There was the man's four-legged stool, on which his children or those who called him 'father' could not sit. There might also be one or more stools for visitors.

(ii) The bedstead was sometimes simply a raised platform of earth, on which specially prepared skins were laid for sleeping on. Mats were also used in places; these were made either of palms (*amalala*) or papyrus.

(iii) The rest of the house was filled up with household utensils and tools. These included pots of all shapes and sizes: *isyongo* for fetching and keeping water; *inungiro* (*liyika*) for cooking meat or fish; *ikhafuka* for making flour-meal (*obusuma*); *olunasulo* or *isatsi* for brewing a little beer; *oluleemo* for brewing much beer; *eshikaye* which was used as a soup plate, and *oluchyo* from which beer was drunk with tubes.

Some of these utensils are not much used today because people prefer to buy pans and plates from the shops.

(iv) There were also various types of baskets: *eshimwero* for carrying things on the head; *omuyinda*, bigger still; *eshiteru* for putting *obusuma* in; *akhalubi*, smaller than *eshiteru*; *akhasowa*, smaller still, used for measuring grain or tobacco in the market; *oluteru*, a large, flat basket used for sifting grain.

There were also calabashes. One type of calabash, *eshisaabo*, was used for storing milk, and also separating it from cream.

The vessel for pounding grain was called *eshinu*. A small *eshinu* was used in some places as *eshisaabo*.

The grinding stone was called *oluchina*, and the smaller stone for crushing grain against this was called *isyo*.

(v) Iron tools included hoes, spears, arrows, knives, and rings for the legs, arms, or neck. Special types of cutting tools were: *ingeso*, a curved knife shaped like a scythe but much smaller; it was generally used for peeling bananas, potatoes and so on. Then there was the *omwolo* which also looked like *ingeso*, but was bigger and thicker, and was attached to a long thick stick. It was used for cutting grass in the field.

8. MEMBERSHIP OF THE CLAN

In lesson 5 we saw something about the family and those who belonged to it. All the members of such a family had responsibilities towards one another. For instance, they shared the meat of a wedding.

Several families like that made up a sub-clan; and several sub-clans made up a clan.

(i) The clan was the most important family unit in the tribe. There are nearly seven hundred and fifty clans in Buluyia.

Each clan has a totem; that is, they have an animal or bird or plant which they do not eat, or which they do not touch. Here are examples of clans and their totems:

Abashitsetse (Wanga): A bushbuck (*imbongo*)
Abamulembo (Bunyala, Busia District): A palm (*olukhindu*)

Each clan swears by its totem. This was done when the person swearing wanted to prove that he or she was not telling a lie. You could not swear by your totem if you knew you were telling a lie as it was believed that the totem would thereby bring you bad luck, or kill you.

In Buluyia, members of one clan do not intermarry. That is why when a Muluyia boy meets a Muluyia girl, the first thing he asks to know, after knowing the name, is what clan the girl belongs to.

Some very big clans with sub-clans, however, sometimes allow intermarriage between the sub-clans. Also, if there was a serious quarrel between the two sub-clans in the far distant past, then no one bothers very much if they intermarry. Cases of this type are very rare. One example is in Maragoli, where the four major sub-clans intermarry, although they all descend from Mulogoli. The example of the Maragoli sub-clans will be given further below.

Most Baluyia clans have family lists which go back more than twelve generations. Some go back as far as thirty generations. You get your family list if you count yourself, then your father, then his father, and so on, backwards till you come to the last person that your old men can remember. Each person in that list will represent a generation.

If you give each generation thirty years, you can find out when the first person lived.

(ii) Here is the family list of the Maragoli clan. In it you can see several sub-clans and family divisions and how they are connected. The Maragoli clan goes back seventeen generations, including the child of one born in 1920. That means that the first person, Muhindira, was born about 500 years ago. The founders of the Maragoli sub-clans, which bear their names, are underlined.

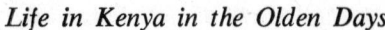

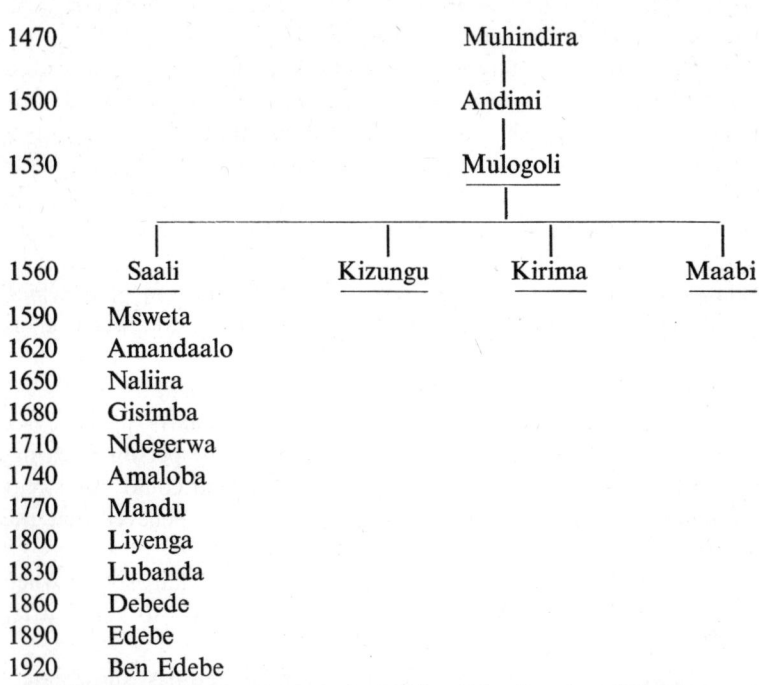

1470	Muhindira
1500	Andimi
1530	Mulogoli
1560	Saali — Kizungu — Kirima — Maabi

1590	Msweta
1620	Amandaalo
1650	Naliira
1680	Gisimba
1710	Ndegerwa
1740	Amaloba
1770	Mandu
1800	Liyenga
1830	Lubanda
1860	Debede
1890	Edebe
1920	Ben Edebe

In the family list we have only followed the lineage of Saali.

After the death of Mulogoli, his sons began to spread gradually to where their sub-clans are today. Saali, Kizungu and Kirima are now found in North Maragoli. Maabi stayed on where his father died, which is now South Maragoli.

Saali had four sons of his own. These four founded the following families, which still bear their names: Abamumbaya, Ababuzuzu, Abasweta and Abamageza. The first two, Mumbaya and Buzuzu, were sons of one wife, while Msweta and Mageza were sons of another wife.

Kizungu had two sons, Gisemba and Aliero, the founders of Abagizemba and Abaliero. Other families which are said to belong to this sub-clan are: Abasuba, Abasaniaga, Abayonga and Abakebembe.

Kirima had four sons: Maseero, Saki, Masingira and Gamuguywa. They too founded the families which bear their names: Abamaseero, Abasaki, Abamasingira and Abagamuguywa.

Maabi, the youngest child, also had four sons: Nondi, Logovo, Nagonda and Mutembe. Nagonda was the youngest of the four. Mutembe was an illegitimate child. The families founded by these four children are Abanondi, Abalogovo, Abagonda and Abamutembe.

The four main sub-clans of Maragoli, namely Abasaali, Abakizungu, Abakirima and Abamaabi, intermarry. That is because they separated such a long time back. But the family groups in each do not intermarry, because they still have strong family connections. A careful study of this Maragoli clan will help you to understand your own and other clans.

(iii) Here are some of the largest clans among the more than 750 clans in Buluyia.

Clan	Where found
Abashitsetse	in Wanga
Abakolwe	in Wanga and Marama
Abakhoone	in western Bunyala, Bukhayo, Bugwe (Uganda), Bunyole (Uganda), Marama, Bukusu, Mfwang'ano Island, etc.
Abamulembo (or Abamulembwa)	in western Bunyala, Wanga, Marach, Ugenya, Samia
Abamilonje	Isukha
Abashiimuli	Idakho
Abayirifuma	Bunyala (Kakamega District)
Abamukhula	Marama
Abamaavi	Maragoli
Abamuteete	Bunyore
Abakitwika	Bukusu
Abafofoyo	Marach
Abaguuri	Bukhayo
Abakhuulo	Bukhekhe
Abatabona	Samia
Abongonya	Butsotso

9. MEMBERSHIP OF THE TRIBE

The Baluyia have many sub-tribes. These will be mentioned further below. Membership of each sub-tribe depends on where one's clan lived. In other words, each sub-tribe is a union of several clans living in continuous territory. The clans need not descend from a single known ancestor. There are some clans which have branches in different sub-tribes (e.g. the Abakhoone). These branches belong to the sub-tribes where they are found. For instance, the Abakhoone in Bukusu are Babukusu, and those in Bunyala are Banyala.

A sub-tribe was and still is distinguished by language (dialect) and its special customs. Also, whenever it was necessary to defend the sub-tribe by going to war, all the members of the clans making up the sub-tribe went willingly to defend their sub-tribe.

(i) *The Sub-Tribes of Buluyia:* The following sub-tribes are found in Buluyia. They are grouped here according to those who have many things in common with each other.

    (*a*) Babukusu
          Ba-Kabras
          Banyala ba Mayero
    (*b*) Abawanga
          Abamarama
          Abatsotso
    (*c*) Abisukha
          Abitakho
          Abalogoli
          Abatiriki
    (*d*) Abanyole
          Abakisa (Abashisa)
    (*e*) Abamarachi
          Abakhayo
    (*f*) Abasamia
          Abakhekhe
          Abanyala
          Abakangala

NOTE: (i) The Abasonga now found in the Nyanza Province are also of Luyia origin and speak Luluyia.

         (ii) There are some Baluyia sub-tribes in Uganda:
            (*a*) Abagisu
            (*b*) Abanyole (Abanyuli)
            (*c*) Abagwe
            (*d*) Abasamia

(ii) *Population:* There are over 1,086,000 Abaluyia in Kenya alone. There are about half that number in Uganda.

(iii) *An Example of a Sub-Tribe:* Let us take the Abakisa (Abashisa) as an example. The sub-tribe consists of the following clans.

(*a*) *Abashisa:* They are an off-shoot of the Abashiimuli of Idakho. The clan has two major sub-clans: Abamase and Abakhunzulu. The Abashisa make the largest clan in Kisa, which is why their name covers the whole sub-tribe.

(*b*) Closely connected with the Abashisa are the *Abashibungo,* who often pass as Abashisa. In fact they are an off-shoot of the Abamwima clan of Wanga.

(c) *Abashirotsa* are an off-shoot of the Abagondi in Idakho and descend from a man called Ebaba.

(d) *Abasamia* descend from a man called Mukitsa who was related to the Abasamia proper, now found in Busia District. The clan consists of five sub-clans: Abakambuli, Abalakayi, Abachero, Abayonga, and Abatayi, founded by the five sons of Mukitsa. Mutayi, the founder of the Abatayi, was the eldest.

(e) *Abakanga* descend from a man called Nasitsi who came from Tiriki. All these clans form the sub-tribe of Kisa.

10. GREETINGS AND HOSPITALITY

(i) *Greetings:* The general greeting in Buluyia is '*Omulembe*', which means 'peace'. This is usually followed by the inquiry, 'What news?'—'*akasungwa*' or '*akaboolwa*'.

In former days shaking hands was done over and over again, like the Baganda do, holding palms and thumbs in alternation for as long as a minute. This type of greeting was usually between friends or relatives who met after parting for a long period of time.

Elders were greeted by saying the words of greeting while raising both palms respectfully towards the forehead, then up and down several times.

Women usually greeted while kneeling and half-sitting on their heels; never when standing up.

Sometimes special greetings were used for different parts of the day. For instance, in the morning they said, '*Bushyere*'. Sometimes they might say, 'How did you sleep?'

During the day they said,'*Akeshiteere?*' or '*Ohonjire orye?*' In the evening it was, '*Bwakheera*' or '*Bwirire*'. The answer to all these was '*Bulayi*' or '*Muno*'.

Younger people always greeted older ones first.

Such greetings were for people who often saw one another.

When people had been separated for a long time, for months or years, other greetings were used. These were different in different areas of Buluyia. Among the western sub-tribes of Buluyia, particularly those in the Busia District, it was '*Khulikhayo*', or '*Khulikha olukendo*'. This is the greeting they use in Buganda, and perhaps these Baluyia got it when they passed through that country some hundreds of years ago.

(ii) *Hospitality:* Within the family, everyone had a right to a share of the food, and to a place to sleep. Those who were well off had a duty to help those who could not help themselves with these necessities of life, in the larger family.

The boys slept in a special hut called *isimba*. There were various names used for it in other areas of Buluyia. *Isimba* is still used by young men in Buluyia, but some now can sleep in their parents' house!

The younger girls and boys slept in their mother's hut. The older girls slept in an old woman's hut called *eshibinzie* in some places. Here they learnt folk tales and other stories of wisdom for girls.

Strangers, too, unless they came from an enemy tribe, had to get food and shelter. It was a sign of ill-breeding to refuse a stranger food. Meals were eaten where everybody present could join in; and everyone was expected to join in without waiting to be asked to do so.

In return, every stranger was expected to behave well in the home, by observing the accepted standards of good behaviour.

11. RULES OF GOOD BEHAVIOUR AND POLITENESS

Such rules were many, and varied from place to place. Here we can only mention those which were common in most places. Some are still observed, others are sometimes disregarded nowadays.

(i) *Behaviour at Meals:*

(*a*) When food was divided out among the children or young people, the older ones were given their share first. Also, they washed their hands first.

(*b*) When cooking or serving food, one had to be careful to keep the food of '*Abasirasi*' apart. '*Abasirasi*' are people who do not eat certain kinds of fish or meat because of taboo or disease.

(*c*) Spitting or blowing the nose, and similar actions were not allowed during meals.

(*d*) Children had to sit flat on the ground. They were not to squat.

(*e*) It was considered a very shameful thing for anyone to eat while another, especially a child, was looking on; or to eat alone.

(*f*) Men ate with men only, including boys of any age. Women ate with other women, and young children of both sexes.

(ii) *Behaviour in the Huts:*

(*a*) Married daughters or sons were not allowed to sleep in or to go to the 'lower side' (or 'fire side') of their parents' sleeping hut, or to shut or open its door.

(*b*) No girls or women sat on men's stools. No boys or men of any age sat on their father's or uncle's special stool.

(iii) *Behaviour towards People:*

(*a*) Parents may not beat their matured daughters.

(*b*) No one may beat or fight his maternal uncle, or any aunt, no matter how young. These and similar relatives were to be respected to the point of fear, in the old days. This custom is still observed.

(c) A great deal of respect was required towards the mother-in-law, and to a certain extent, the father-in-law. In some places one was not to meet his mother-in-law; and, of course, he could never eat with her. This custom is not so rigidly observed nowadays.

On the other hand, people were expected to be much more free with their sisters-in-law. (Except in Isukha and Idakho, where these are still treated like parents-in-law).

(d) All older people were to be respected and given priority by their juniors. For instance, the oldest son always married before other sons, and the oldest daughter before the other daughters. This is changing!

(e) Young people, however, were encouraged to crack jokes with those they called grandfather or grandmother; also with great-aunts and great-uncles.

(f) No one may laugh at a lame person.

(g) One may not beat a person he is chasing if the latter enters anyone's house, or seeks refuge at the back of the pursuer's mother or aunt.

(h) At a beer party, one may not pass above drinking tubes or people's legs.

(iv) *General Responsibility:*

(a) Everyone had a duty to help his neighbour who was in trouble, or to save another's property which was in danger.

(b) For instance, everyone had a duty to help anyone drowning, or whose hut was burning, or whose crops were being destroyed by animals, and so on.

(c) Honesty was considered very important. A person who was not honest, even in small ways, was despised by others, and often he was avoided.

Because of changed conditions in this country many of these good rules are unfortunately not so rigidly followed today.

Chapter 3

Clothing of Long Ago

1. CLOTHES WORN BY MEN

Luyia men used to wear the prepared skin of a goat or a calf. It was passed under one armpit and fastened with a strap over the opposite shoulder. The skin, hung in this position, was not sufficient to cover the whole body; what the man did was to shift it every time to cover that part of the body which faced the people he was supposed to 'fear' (respect). These included mothers-in-law, aunts and all women he called 'mother'.

In addition to this skin, the wealthier people put on other items of dress. For instance, a chief had a special cap (*shimwata*) which was covered with a small animal's skin and decorated with beads or cowrie shells. Sometimes they also wore a leopard's skin, and a royal bangle (*omukasa*) on their wrists. Ordinary men wore iron rings (*ebitiiri*) on their ankles and legs; richer ones might wear *emisanga* (bands of twisted wire).

2. THOSE WORN BY WOMEN

The women used to wear *liboya*, made of banana fibres or sisal or, for richer women (*abakhaye*), of animals' tail hairs. The *liboya* was worn round the waist and looked like a kind of apron hanging in front and a tuft of sisal or hair strings hanging behind. It was a very important dress and had to be respected according to custom.

The women also wore strings of beads round their waists and necks. Cowrie shells arranged artistically on a leather strap were also sometimes worn round the neck by older women. The women also wore *ebitiiri* on their ankles. And some wore other rings and wire round their necks or on their arms. They liked decorating themselves: some made holes in their ear lobes for putting in decorations; others tattooed their bodies—usually the forehead, the abdomen and the back.

At a dance they tied little bells (*tsindeke*) round their ankles and legs.

3. THOSE WORN BY CHILDREN

Young girls only wore strings of beads round their waists and necks and pierced their ear lobes to put in little decorations. When they got older they tattooed themselves. This was done artistically on the forehead, back, chest and abdomen. There were many symmetrical shapes: circles or half-circles, zigzag lines, even figures of animals.

Young boys either went naked, or used a wide strap of leather as *eshikhonera*. It was attached to a string round the waist and passed between the thighs to be fixed on the string again on the other side of the body.

4. THOSE WORN ON SPECIAL OCCASIONS

During war men painted themselves with frightening colours, and wore frightening apparel such as horns. On a festive occasion they also painted themselves, though differently. Often they wore headdresses decorated with feathers of ostriches (*amaudo*) or with skins of the Colobus monkey (*ituru*).

On very ceremonial occasions such as going to the funeral of one's mother-in-law, leading a procession after one has killed a leopard or lion, or leading a procession after one is made chief, the man concerned wore a very special headgear (*ishimbishira*). This consisted of a conical cap (often called *eshitwetwe*) which was decorated with cowrie shells, and had, sticking out of its apex, an upright short or long stick at the tip of which was a tuft of rare feathers—of a little rare bird called *ishimbishira*.

Medicine-men liked putting on impressive attire according to their personal taste. And they often advised their patients to wear lucky charms (*amairisi*) and similar items.

5. PREPARATION OF SKINS

After skinning an animal, the skin was spread and pegged on the ground with its flesh side up. Then the pieces of meat were carefully removed. Hair, too, was gradually removed. This first part of the job was done by men. Then the skin was handed to women who first soaked it in a special solution; when it was ready they rubbed it and rinsed it until it was clear of all dirt. Sometimes pieces were sewn together by using a little bone as a needle and sinews as thread.

The final result was a soft skin, called *ingubo* in many places, which was highly valued. Only rich adult people could afford to wear this type of skin.

The skins for sleeping on were not prepared so laboriously.

6. BARKCLOTH (OMUKOKHO)

This was an industry native to the Bantu tribes of Uganda. Those living close to Lake Victoria knew how to make it out of the bark and sap of a certain tree called *omuduubu*. But the barkcloth from Buganda and Busoga was much better made and those who wanted to buy the barkcloth preferred to buy the imported ones which were brought by Busoga traders across Berkeley Bay. So local makers of barkcloth eventually stopped making it.

NOTE

In Buluyia the climate was warm or hot and there was no real need for clothes. Tribes living in cold areas, for instance the Kikuyu, had to wear heavier skins to keep themselves warm.

Chapter 4

Buying and Selling

1. IN THE OLD DAYS

(i) *Exchange:* Before the Europeans came, there was no money in Buluyia. People bought and sold things by exchange.

A goat was sold for two or three hoes. A bull was sold for three goats; a cow for four goats and so on. There were slight variations in different places where goats and hoes were plentiful.

(ii) *Measures:* Grain was measured according to the type and size of basket. Some of these were mentioned in Chapter 2, when dealing with furniture and utensils. Apart from the granary, the *omuyinda*, the largest type of basket, was the biggest measure. This, when full, could not be carried by one person. In fact, it was generally accepted that when full the *omuyinda* contained enough grain for three people to carry. The *eshimwero* was the next size of basket. It was this that the women carried on their heads. On the average *eshimwero* can hold between 30 and 40 pounds of millet, whereas *omuyinda* can hold 100 or more pounds.

Smaller basket measures included the *akhamyero* (a small basket) and the *eshiteru* (smaller still). The *oluteru* was a flat wide basket and measured unshelled millet. The smallest basket measure was *akhasowa*, which dished out small quantities of millet when selling on a retail basis. This measure is still common in African markets; nowadays some are very small and flat because of the high prices.

There were also liquid measures for things like milk, porridge and beer. These were various types and sizes of pots and calabashes.

Tobacco was tied in an oval bundle called *olushisi*.

(iii) *Buying by 'Pledge' (omusingo):* This was a kind of hire purchase, commonly used when buying grain or meat during difficult times. A person who had plenty of grain would give it out in definite measures to people whom he or she knew well; they would then repay this at a fixed time, usually during the next harvest or period of plenty. This was similarly applied to meat, fish, tobacco and other commodities.

(iv) *Going to the Market in Old Days (Okhusuma):* Usually it was not necessary to go to the market to buy anything. People usually bought and sold what they wanted within the village. If you wanted tobacco or grain, you went to the women who were known to have plenty of it, and so on.

During times of scarcity of food or a full-scale famine, it was necessary to travel long distances to reach a market. The markets were few and far removed, and they only functioned during periods of scarcity of food.

The journey to the market was full of hazards; so people from one *olukongo* used to travel in a large caravan. It was not easy for wild animals or hostile people to attack such a large group. Such a journey was, of course, done on foot, and it took many days before the caravan returned with the grain they had gone to buy.

(v) *New Ideas and New Friends:* Such trips opened the minds of the villagers to new ideas, through contact with foreign tribesmen. Many useful friendships began to develop: the caravan might sleep in a friendly foreigner's home, and this might lead to an exchange visit later. This relationship often led to a girl of the one group being married in the other, which helped to cement the relationship and make it lasting.

(vi) *People Sold in Exchange for Food:* If there was a real famine, it sometimes happened that a man might exchange his daughter for food. Usually he exchanged her with rich strangers with whom he had become acquainted. After the famine the friendship would usually continue, and the girl would remain married where she was exchanged for food.

Boys were also sold in temporary and permanent slavery as a result of famines.

Sometimes young men and women were given in exchange for food when the owners of the food would accept nothing else. But in many other cases, the parents of young boys and girls gave them out merely to get them into a home where they could get a meal and so survive the famine.

(vii) *Things Sold in a Market:* As has already been said, the main item sold in a market was food, usually in the form of grain. But those who came to buy it brought what they had to exchange. These included iron implements and weapons like knives, axes, spears, shields, and hoes; household utensils like baskets, pots, dishes; furniture like stools; items of dress like prepared skins, bark cloth, beads, bangles, ceremonial hats and caps; poultry, including tamed birds such as quails; cattle, sheep and goats—wanted mainly in connection with 'bride price'; medicines of all descriptions; and many other such items.

(viii) *Expenses on the way to and from the Market:* A caravan travelling to a distant market often had to pay fees in order to pass through the *tsingongo* on their way. People who claimed to come from the *olukongo* of a well-known and friendly chief were often allowed to pass without charge, and they were also given much help. Those from the *olukongo* of a hostile chief would be robbed or captured. This led to considerable importance being given to one's chief. In many cases people had to report to their chief before they left for a distant market. He expected them to give him a present for his co-operation.

2. BUYING AND SELLING TODAY

Today most of the things mentioned under number (vii) above are brought to the markets to be sold for money. There are many markets now and not very far removed from each other. Most people live within easy reach of a market. If they want to go to distant markets, they can do so without fear and without having to walk—as it is possible to use a bicycle, a bus or a train.

There is no need to describe an African market of today; the best way of learning about it is to visit one and observe what is bought and sold.

Chapter 5

How People Told the Time

1. HOURS
There were six main divisions of a day of twenty-four hours. These were:
- (i) *Itsuli:* morning
- (ii) *Musiteere:* during the day when the sun is high
- (iii) *Musitsyambo:* afternoon, including early evening
- (iv) *Mungolobe:* evening (after dark)
- (v) *Mushiro* (*Butukhu*)*:* in the night
- (vi) *Mumasherebende:* from cockcrow to sunrise

2. Each of these six divisions had the following smaller divisions:
- (i) *Itsuli:*
  - (a) *Elyuba nilirula:* at sunrise
  - (b) *Musenya:* in the morning, from 7 a.m. to 10 a.m. (N.B. There are several divisions of *musenya* known locally; these should be taught)
- (ii) *Musiteere:*
  - (a) *Mumabolola ke tsing'ombe:* when cattle are going to graze
  - (b) *Mumakakula:* at lunch time, 12:00
  - (c) *Musiteere hakari:* midday, about 1:00 p.m.
- (iii) *Musitsyambo:*
  - (a) *Mumang'wesia ke tsing'ombe:* when the cows go to drink at the river or pool, about 3:00 p.m.
  - (b) *Mumakeresya ke tsing'ombe:* when the cows are going back home, about 5:00 p.m.
  - (c) *Tsingokho nitsinjira:* when the chickens enter the house, about 6:00 p.m.
- (iv) *Mungolobe:*
  - (a) *Elyuba nilikwa:* at sunset, about 6:30 p.m.
  - (b) *Musisisye:* at twilight, about 7:00 p.m.

(c) *Mumabutsa:* during conversation time, 7:30 to 9:00 p.m.
   (d) *Mumeyalisya:* at bedtime, about 9:30 p.m.
 (v) *Musiro (Butukhu):*
   (a) *Esyalo nisinyiranyiraane:* when the world is quiet, about 10:30 p.m.
   (b) *Mundoolo tsya mabeere:* during the 'milky' sleep, about 11:00 p.m.
   (c) *Mushisimukho shyamberi:* at the first waking, about 11:30 p.m.
   (d) *Mushiro hakari:* in the middle of the night, about 12:00 to 2:00 a.m.
   (e) *Mushisimukho shyokhubiri:* at the second waking, about 2:00 to 3:00 a.m.
 (vi) *Mumasherebende:*
   (a) *Mungokho tsyambere:* at the first cock crow, 3:00 a.m.
   (b) *Masherebende:* at the early hour, 4:00 a.m.
   (c) *Mungokho tsyanyuma:* at the second crow, 5:00 a.m.
   (d) *Ebukwe niyisheba:* when the east begins to clear, about 5:30 a.m.
   (e) *Mumabwibwi:* just before sunrise, about 6:00 a.m. (also called *Amayoni nikemba:* when the birds are singing)

3. THE DAYS OF THE WEEK

All Baluyia had names for six days of the week. The Banyala be Mumbo had, in addition, a name for Sunday; it is included in this list.

Monday	Olwe imberi	the first day
	or Olwe-ibarasa	the day for tribal meetings
	or Olwakhurula omulimo	when work starts
Tuesday	Olwakhabiri	the second day
Wednesday	Olwakhataru	the third day
	or Olwakhabaka	
Thursday	Olwakhane	the fourth day
Friday	Olwakharanu	the fifth day
Saturday	Olwakhasasaba	the sixth day
	or Olweinyongesa	the additional day
Sunday	Olwomudiira	the day for 'holding back', for not working.

4. TELLING THE TIME BY THE MOON

The Baluyia recognized the four quarters of the moon. These quarters had various names in the different parts of Buluyia. Here the terms used in western Buluyia are used. Schools in other areas should substitute these with local terms.

First Quarter: *Omwosi kulabire* (the moon has become light)

Half Moon: *Omwosi kuli hekulu* (the high moon)

Full Moon: *Omwosi kudola indukusi* (the moon that picks up a very small insect—i.e. very bright)

Last Quarter: *Omwosi kwe igweli* (the moon that is in the form of a crescent)

5. MONTHS

Each full cycle of the above four appearances made up a month. There were thirteen months altogether. One of them (between June and July) was very short and can be omitted. These months often had only local names, especially in eastern Buluyia. In western Buluyia, however, the following names were used.

January	*Dulienge*
February	*Wefu*
March	*Muungu:* during which many people usually died. The word comes from *Okhuunga* which means 'crazy'.
April	*Mwerasi*
May	*Nangeka:* the month of much rain and black clouds. This was a month of green grass, plenty of food; floods; and fish were available.
June	*Musaru*
(Extra Month)	*Unondaye:* literally, 'where are you following me to?' This was a harsh reproach by a woman to her little child who would follow her into someone else's garden where she was going to pinch cowpeas (*tsing'oli*). The full expression is, '*Unondaye mung'oli tsyabene?*'
July	*Munane:* This does not mean 'eight'. It comes from '*okhwenaana*' which means to implore ceaselessly, to press an unresponsive person. The people wanted rain to ripen their crops, but there was none in this month.
August	*Fulula:* the harvest month
September	*Namafumbye:* the cloudy month. *Lifumbi* is 'cloudiness'.
October	*Ofwomoole:* the month of sudden floods.
November	*Mubiru*
December	*Olusisi:* the final month. (Each granary is tied with rings. The bottom-most ring is called *olusisi*. This is where the name comes from.)

6. THE SEASONS AND LONGER PERIODS OF TIME
There were three main seasons in the year:
Esiminyu: the dry season, December to February.
Irotso: the rain season, April to June.
Esirumbi: the short rains, September to November.
For farming purposes, the following activities made up special seasons:
Lilima: cultivation time, December to February.
Liraka: sowing time, February to March.
Elyaka: weeding time, April.
Likesa: harvest time, July to August.
Esirumbi: second crop, September to November.
In eastern Buluyia they differ slightly due to different climatic conditions.
The year is *omuhika*. Longer periods of time were decided in one of two ways: either they used age-groups, or they remembered the major events.

Thus they would say, 'It happened when so-and-so was a baby', or when he was 'able to fetch fire', or when he was *omusoliri*, and so on. These age-groups were dealt with in Chapter 2. You should go back to them. If you wish you might make a time chart of a school child's life in preparation for the next lesson.

7. CALCULATING TIME FROM MAJOR EVENTS
The major events which were used included famines, wars, epidemics, droughts, major floods, and so on. Naturally, most of these occurred in different places at different times, and were thus given local names.

Here is an example of how people remembered time in Samia and Bunyala during the last two hundred years. The dates have been worked out by using known family lists as explained earlier, in the lesson on Membership of the Clan. People of various clans were concerned in these events and their family lists have been carefully checked to arrive at these approximate dates. (Note: these should be taught in more than one lesson in western Buluyia. In eastern Buluyia they should only serve as an example for teaching more local dates where available.)

1750	The wars of 'Odende', 'Khagono' and 'Ndong'a', which were fought between the people of a certain area of Bunyala and the Luo people of Alego. These were names of people who figured most in these wars.
1750–1770	Various wars in what is now Bunyala (Buongo) between Abakhoone and Abasamia and between Abasinyama and Abasamia. In these wars some of the Banyala of the Kakamega District were forced to migrate from Bunyala Buongo.

1770–1780	Formation of the six well-known war groups in Bunyala today; namely, Abamukwambo, Abakhuuri, Abalwang'a, Abapondi, Abaofu and Abarula. Also the formation of the four major war-groups in Samia; namely, Ababburi, Abadongo, Abatabona and Abakhuulo.
1780–1800	Various wars between the above Bunyala groups and the above Samia groups.
1800	All the above groups fight against the large and fierce Abakhoone clan in the great War of 'Ifunikho' or 'Eshiatikho' (Migration). The Abakhoone and clans sympathizing with them were sent out of Bunyala and Samia. Many of them went to Bugwe in Uganda. Some of these latter left Bugwe for Bunyala in the Kakamega District. As a result of this great war, the Abakhoone clan was scattered and are found in Bukusu (Namajanja's family), in Bukhayo, Marama, Bunyole (Uganda), Bugwe, etc.
1810–1830	Various battles against the remaining Basamia in Bunyala.
1840	The great war of 'Obuyu' by the Banyala against the Luos of Alego. The Banyala took Usonga in this war.
1840–1850	The great famine of 'Lumala' (destruction) in which thousands died.
1850	The recall of some Abakhoone back to Bunyala. The people feared that the famine was a punishment from God for expelling Abakhoone.
1870	The war of 'Odembo' against Samia.
1875	The war of 'Madara'—Samia against Abakhekhe. In this war the people of Busoga (Uganda) took part.

8. MORE RECENT DATES

(These should be taught in all Luyia schools.)

1875	The first European, H. M. Stanley, touched Buluyia on his voyage round Lake Victoria. He landed at Igoye and near Port Victoria in the Berkeley Bay.
1883	(November-December) Arrival of the first European to pass through Buluyia on foot—Joseph Thomson. From Kabaras he visited Mumia who gave him guides to take him to the mouth of the River Nzoia in Bunyala. He heard and wrote about the war of Madara, already mentioned. He went back through Ochembo's home in Samia and Odunga's home in Bukhayo. He reached and named Mt. Elgon. In Bukusu he saw that a

	Swahili slave trader called Sudi had burnt many villages and killed many people.
1885	The locust raid of 'Osodo' in Samia.
1890	The famine of 'Oswekha' in Samia.
1894	The war of 'Lumboka' in Bukusu.
1895	The war of 'Chetambe' in Bukusu.
1908	The famine of 'Demesi' in Kakamega District.
	The famine of 'Achoka' in west Buluyia.
1918	The famine of 'Ngaira' in Kakamega District. Ngaira was a rainmaker who died.
1918	The famine of 'Obando' in west Buluyia. 'Obando' is maize flour in Luo. Maize flour was sold for the first time in this famine.
1927	The famine of 'Liboyi' in Kakamega District.
1941	The famine of bananas—when people went to work in Maragoli to get bananas.
1943	The famine of 'Shikombe' in Kakamega and Bungoma Districts; or the famine of 'Kedereyo' in Busia District. The government helped people and schools to get cassava and millet.
1953	The famine of Mau Mau.

Chapter 6

Hunting

1. HUNTING TRADITIONS

(i) Hunting was very common in the old days. Often people hunted to get meat. But in other cases they hunted to keep away the wild animals which destroyed their crops. In this second case hunting was an important affair of a village or *olukongo*. Every adult man in the area was expected to join in. Even in the case of hunting for the sake of getting meat, only few people stayed at home.

A signal for hunting was given early in the morning by blowing the horn in a particular manner. All the strong men then came out with their spears, knives and dogs. In some areas bows and arrows were used also.

There were definite rules for hunting, and everyone was expected to follow them strictly. This was to avoid accidents such as someone piercing another with his spear or arrow. Also, such discipline made it possible for those who speared the animal to get their rightful share of the meat.

The dogs had bells (*bikhule* or *amabwobo*) round their necks so that their whereabouts could be known. A dog which co-operated in killing an animal got its share of the meat.

(ii) In some parts of Buluyia the first person to hit the animal with his spear or arrow shouted, 'I am the first' and claimed the biggest share of the meat. The number of marks on the animal also added to the amount of meat one got.

In west Buluyia the practice was slightly different. A person who speared first shouted out the symbol of his clan. For instance, the Abakhoone said, '*Ndikho ndi gonza*'; the Abamulembo said, '*Ndikho ndi omurwa owarula siongo nyama*'; the Abadongo said, '*Ndikho ndi rachiebo*', and so on. After killing the animal, the members of his clan shared the meat according to a rule. This was slightly different in different areas, and you should find out what applies to your area. If a member of another clan also speared the animal before it died, he too would get a definite share.

(iii) Hunting was sometimes done by digging pits or making traps. Pits were useful for killing huge animals like the hippopotamus or fierce ones like the leopard. A large pit was dug and a thin covering sprinkled with soil or grass was put on its mouth. When necessary, a bait was put nearby. The unsuspecting animal was then easily caught. The people finished it off by spearing it the next morning.

Traps or snares were many, and varied from place to place. A popular one was that of a huge stone with an attached spear blade pointing downwards, which hung at a convenient height on the narrow path of the desired animal. The stone was secured to the ground by a rope which acted as a kind of lever or pulley. The slightest touch on this rope or string brought the huge stone down with the spear into the body of the animal. This trap was called *likenga* in some areas.

Other animals were caught by using nets made of strings. Birds were sometimes caught by the loop of a string which was attached to a bent branch capable of springing up when touched. Children caught birds by using the latter method, as well as by using a vegetable sticking-paste which they applied on blades of grass.

(iv) The animals commonly hunted in the different parts of Buluyia included the following:

Bush buck	*Imbongo*	Hippo	*Ifubu*
Gazelle	*Eshitsusu*	Rhino	*Amuga*
Warthog	*Injiri*	Buffalo	*Imboko*
Thomson's Gazelle	*Ajili*	Eland	*Ikhulo*
		Elephant	*Inzofu*

The smaller animals like the mole (*ifukho*), the squirrel (*nakhamuna*), and the hare (*esituyu*) were hunted by children.

The birds hunted included the guinea fowl (*likhanga*), the quail (*isindu*) water ducks (*amayoyo*), and many other water birds and tree birds.

The children were more interested in smaller birds such as the weaver-bird, and the bird called *ikherekete* which looks like a chicken but is smaller.

2. HOW HUNTERS LIVED

The Baluyia hunted animals, but they also cultivated the land. There are other tribes which lived only by hunting, such as the Dorobo.

3. TWO HUNTING STORIES

You can tell this or another hunting story. This short story shows that in some hunts the hunters were not so lucky and they killed no animals.

It also tells something about the character of the sort of man who remained at home while others went to a hunt. The story goes like this:

One day the people blew their horns and the men went to a bushy area to hunt. It was a very hot day. The people tried their best, but they killed no animals. They saw a few squirrels and hares but no bucks. When the time for lunch passed, many people were getting tired of the hunt. Some began to steal away back home.

One of these hurried to the nearest hut because he was very thirsty and he wanted some water to drink. Now the owner of the house was a mean person, who ate with no one except his wife, and even refused to go to a village hunt.

As the hunter approached the hut, he saw that the man and his wife were just starting to eat. When they saw him, the wife hid the steaming food (*obusuma*) in a hurry behind some pots, but the hunter pretended not to see this.

He entered the hut, greeted them, mumbled something about the hot weather, and then sat down. The husband and wife did not seem to want him to stay, but he did not mind.

Then the husband asked him about the hunt. This pleased the hunter, who told them about some funny incidents during the hunt. One of them was this: 'I missed one warthog very narrowly. It came from my right towards my left. I waited until it was straight ahead of me, just as far as where the steaming *obusuma* is.' As he said this, he pointed at the food they had hidden. 'I threw my spear but, unfortunately, I missed it'. The man and his wife laughed no more. They realized he had seen them hiding the food, and they were very ashamed. So they brought out the food and ate it with him.

Another Hunting Story: One day Ojwolijwoli (the wise hare) went to the elephant and said, 'I am going somewhere for a visit tomorrow, but I have no buttock. Could you lend me yours and I shall return it after the visit?'

The elephant did not like the idea. But Ojwolijwoli pressed him hard with much argument, explaining that there was no harm to the elephant if the part of its body was cut away temporarily. In the end the elephant very reluctantly agreed. And Ojwolijwoli cut away the part and took it home.

Of course he was not going to pay anyone a visit. He just roasted the meat and ate it over a number of days. The elephant waited for two days, three days, four days, but Ojwolijwoli did not appear as he had promised. The elephant developed a big wound full of maggots where the flesh had been cut.

Hunting

In the end he sent a buck, Nambongo, to find out what had happened. When Nambongo told Ojwolijwoli the story, Ojwolijwoli said, 'That is all right. I shall give it to you. But first I must give you something to eat, as you have travelled a long way and must be tired and hungry.'

Then Ojwolijwoli cooked part of the meat he had cut from the elephant. The meat tasted delicious, and Nambongo asked where it could be found. And Ojwolijwoli answered that the animals from which he got such nice meat were plentiful on a nearby hill. If Nambongo wanted to kill one, Ojwolijwoli would be glad to take him to the hill for the purpose. Nambongo wanted to, so they went.

When they got there, Ojwolijwoli told Nambongo to stay down while he himself went higher up. He said, 'Stay here and watch, and when you hear a little noise, 'Ndiiiiiii', do not do anything. But when you hear a heavy noise, look down and stick your horns forward and they will kill the animal.'

Ojwolijwoli then went up and threw several small stones, which made the little noise, 'Ndiiiiii.' Then he pushed a huge stone and let it roll towards Nambongo. The latter looked down and stuck out his horns ready to kill the animal. But the stone crushed him to death, and Ojwolijwoli made meat of him. This happened to all the messengers whom the elephant sent one after the other.

4. THINGS FOUND BY HUNTING

Let the children suggest first; then explain.

Meat was the most important one. Then there were the skins which were used for a number of purposes. Some were used for sleeping on, for instance, that of the buffalo. Others provided flat strapped shoes for protection against thorns. Yet others were worn as dresses or decorations, for instance, that of the Colobus monkey (its skin is called *ituru* in western Buluyia). Colourful robes and headgears were made out of this.

Rare articles were made out of other things like the hairs of the tails of the giraffe (*obutiga*), which made rare bracelets worn round the ankles, the wrists and the neck by women.

The tail of the zebra (*imbwori*) was a rare and expensive fly-whisk used only by chiefs and famous medicine-men.

The feathers of certain birds, too, were much sought after. For instance, the feathers of the ostrich (*amawudo*), and those of a little, rare bird with long tail feathers called *isimbikhira*. The latter was used in western Buluyia on ceremonial headgears which were used only on the most honoured occasions such as going in procession to the funeral of a mother-in-law or father-in-law; or when one has killed a lion or leopard. We saw about this when dealing with dress in Chapter 3.

The ivory of warthogs, hippos, and even elephants, was used for making a crescent-like article (*igweli*), which was worn by elderly men on the forehead as a sign of riches and power.

Other articles, like horns, were worn for decoration on happy occasions.

Medicine-men and witchdoctors got many articles useful for their trade from dead animals. The fat of a lion is still used as a famous medicine for rubbing into the body. The claws of birds and animals were much used by witchdoctors, as also other parts of an animal's body.

Draw some of the articles and objects mentioned in the above lesson.

5. OTHER THINGS FOUND

(i) *Fish:* Fishing was a special type of hunting. It was an important occupation among the Baluyia living close to Lake Victoria and the lower valleys of Rivers Nzoia, Sio and Yala. Two sub-tribes in Buluyia were particularly famous as fishermen: the Banyala of Buongo, and the Abasamia of Samia.

In the old days they used fishing traps of different kinds, for instance, the following:

Olukhwira: made of reeds plaited with ropes and then built in a special manner along seasonal river valleys, or along the lake side where water is not too deep. Once fish entered it, they could not get out. They were then either speared or caught by smaller traps.

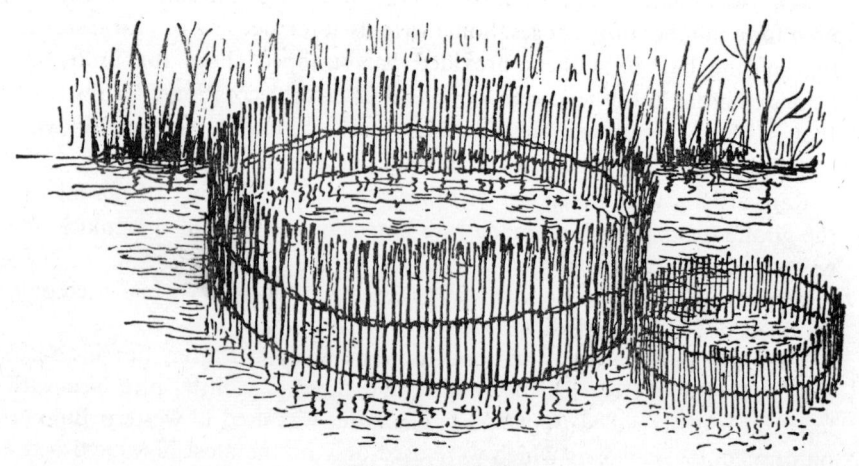

OLUKHWIRA

Hunting

Omukono: This was a trap made of sticks and ropes which was sometimes put in *olukhwira* to catch fish entering there. Also, once fish got into it, they could not get out.

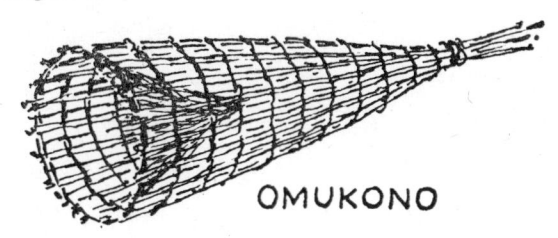

OMUKONO

Obulalo: This was a structure built with poles across a river. On top it was sometimes used as a bridge, while below the *omukono* traps were put in to catch fish.

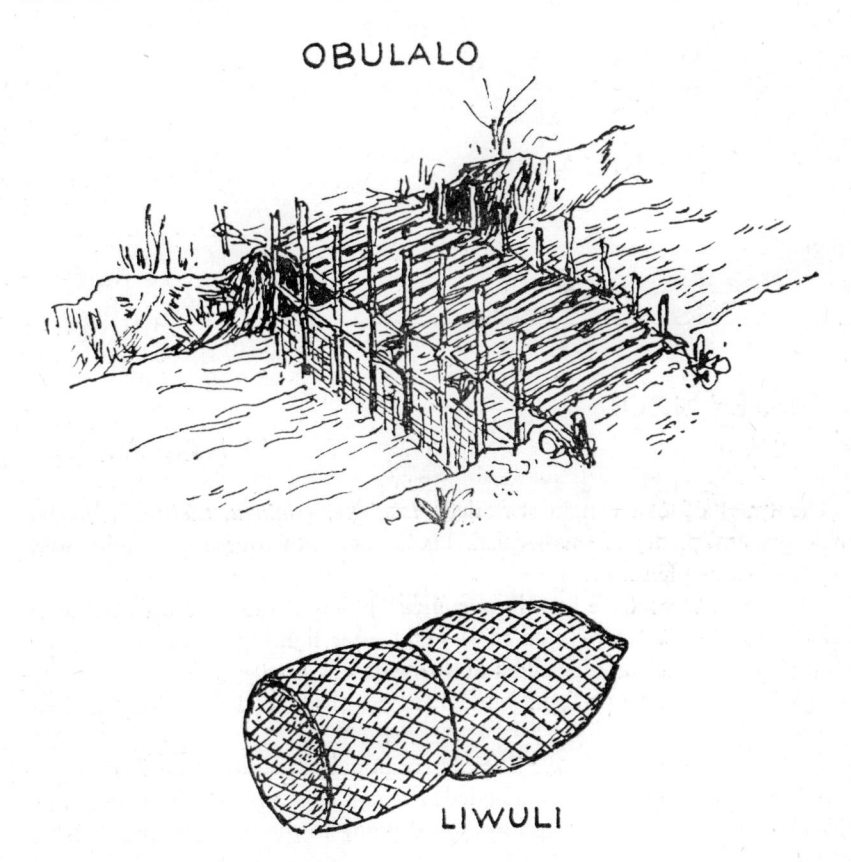

OBULALO

LIWULI

Liwuli: These were made of papyrus and arranged in a pattern in waist-deep lake water like a seine (*likokhoolo*). They caught plenty of fish.

Women used the following traps: *esiwu, esibamo, olubanzo* and *ikhafwa.*

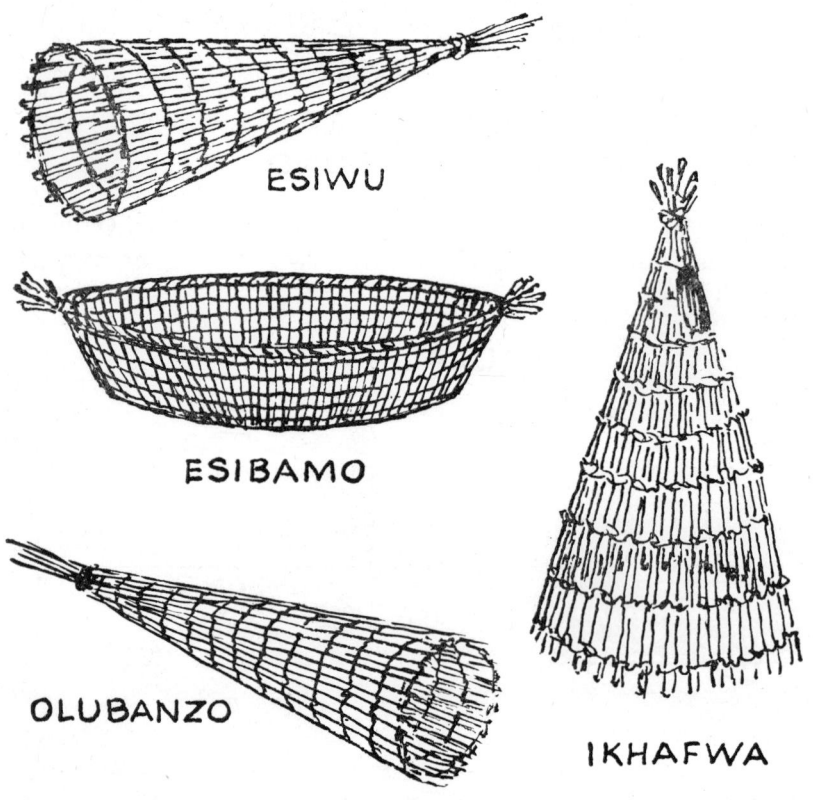

ESIWU

ESIBAMO

OLUBANZO

IKHAFWA

The types of fish caught included: *tsingeke, tsiningu, tsisiire, ebidonge, tsimonye,* and plenty of smaller fish. These names, of course, were only used where fish was plentiful.

(ii) *Honey:* Bees were kept in *omulinga* or they made their own home in a tree or cave. Honey was taken at night after lighting a fire close to the bee-hive. The bees were harmless in this way.

In addition to being a food, honey was also used as a medicine for chest diseases.

(iii) *Plants and Wild Fruit:* These were popular, but different in different areas. Some of the wild fruits included: *tsinduli, emisaali, emikhuwa, eminugu* and *otsyoga.* Girls and young boys loved going to the bush to collect these.

Hunting

Roots were used as medicines.

The sap of certain trees, for instance cacti and euphorbia, was heated and turned into a kind of 'gum' for sticking knives, axes and spears into their wooden handles.

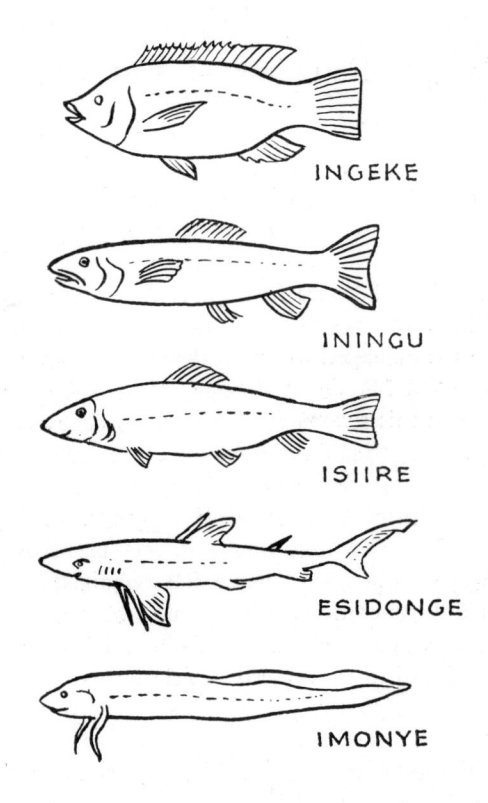

INGEKE

ININGU

ISIIRE

ESIDONGE

IMONYE

Chapter 7

Some Famous Founders of Clans in Buluyia

1. MAYERO

During the days when the Baluyia were crossing from Uganda to their present home in Buluyia, they had a famous leader called Mayero. Mayero was a tall and brave man who was a very devoted leader of his people. He is remembered especially because he organized the crossing of the swamps of Lake Kyoga. There were no boats, but the thousands of men, women and children whom he led managed to travel through the wide, muddy swamp safely, till they reached Ibanda in Busoga. There were several groups of Baluyia which crossed this swamp, and Mayero is believed to have led the very first of these groups, which shows how brave he was. It was such a long time ago that people do not remember much of what he did. Much of what is told of him is in the form of legends or wise sayings. When people want to say that someone lived a very long time ago, they usually say, 'He crossed (the lake) with Mayero'. Mayero's name has remained in many parts of Buluyia and for many generations children have been named after him. In some parts of Buluyia people say that Mayero used to work miracles; in such places he is referred to as Makero, which means 'very strange'.

2. MASIRIBAYI AND HIS SON MAYERO

Masiribayi was the founder of the Abayirifuma clan of Bunyala in Kakamega District. Masiribayi is believed to have come from Uasin Gishu or Trans Nzoia, and he may either have been of Masai or Kalenjin origin. (The Baluyia called the Masai Abakwabi or Abaseebe, and they called the Kalenjin Abarwa or Abatwa).

Masiribayi came with his cattle and pitched a home at Sang'aalo. He found there the clan known as Abasonge. After a short stay at Sang'aalo, he left his cattle with the chief of Abasonge and crossed the River Sio to Bugwe in Uganda. There he lived near Busia, in the home of the chief of the area called Musaya. He married and bore a son called Mayero, whom he named after the ancient leader of Abaluyia.

Masiribayi died before he could come back to Sang'aalo. But it is said that his friend, Musaya, bequeathed his ruling powers to Mayero. It was this Mayero who led the clans now in Bunyala (Kakamega District) back to the Kenya side of River Sio. He did not reach Bunyala, as the movement took several generations because they often settled at one place for a long time before moving again. His great-grandson, Ndombi, became the first big leader when they reached present-day Bunyala. The Banyala used to call the forest which still borders their country *olukaka lwa Mayero* because it acted as a fence to protect them during wars.

3. KASAMU OF IDAKHO

There is an important clan in Idakho called Abashiimuli. Its founder was a man called Kasamu. Like Masiribayi, he is believed to have come from the direction of Uasin Gishu. He too first arrived at Sang'aalo and lived for a time among the Abasonge. Later he moved on with his cattle and family to Butsotso. His wife was called Ashiimuli. After some time Kasamu moved again, this time to Idakho. But one of his sons remained in Butsotso where he founded the clan known as Abashibuli.

When Kasamu reached Idakho he found there Ndunde, chief of the Abakisiira clan. Ndunde welcomed him happily, but soon Kasamu played him a trick and took his chieftainship, so that today the Abashiimuli are the ruling clan in Idakho.

Apart from the son who remained in Butsotso, Kasamu had four other sons: Anasio, Andaye, Mulongo and Butukhu. These sons became the founders of the four sub-clans of the Abashiimuli in Idakho.

4. CHIBOLOLI OF ISUKHA

The founder of the Abamilonje, the largest clan in Isukha today, was a man called Chibololi. He is also believed to have come from Uasin Gishu, and is thought to have been Omukwabi (Masai). His full name was Chibololi arap Roti. Sometimes he is called other names in Isukha.

Some people were hostile to him in Uasin Gishu so he escaped and found his way to Mushyeyu or Bukhungu, now called Kakamega. Then he moved on till he came to *Ikhonga Murwi*, a tall granite stone that appears to have a head, near the road between Kakamega and Mukumu.

Here he was discovered by some women and children. The men thought of killing him. But Chibololi ran to someone's village and picked up a baby and held it in his arms. This meant that, according to custom, they could not kill him now. So the men spared him and gave him the name of Omwitsa.

He lived in someone's home for a few months, but then it was discovered that he had made a girl of the home pregnant. This was a bad crime. The people said he had to pay a cow or else they would kill him. Now Chibololi had no cow or anything. So he escaped back to Uasin Gishu, and came back with his father and the whole of their family. His father paid the cow which the people wanted and thanked them for looking after his son. So they were allowed to stay in peace. They were given a neglected piece of land near Kakamega where lepers used to be isolated. Chibololi and his family worked hard and made the area very productive.

They were very talkative and sometimes told lies, so they were given the name of Abamilionje, which later became Abamilonje.

5. OKURO OF BUKHEKHE

One of the ancestors of the Abakhulo clan in Bukhekhe was a man called Okuro son of Asa. Okuro's great-grandfather, Olando, had once lived near Mt. Elgon (Masaaba) and then moved on to Ibanda. Olando's grandson Asa moved on to Igoye Bay in the present Yimbo location of the Luos. It was from here that his son Okuro moved to Kadenge where he lived with the Luo leader, Owiny Sigoma. Owiny was a treacherous old man and Okuro escaped his evil tricks only by chance.

It happened when Okuro had gone to hunt guinea fowls as usual in the Gafumbulire area. Owiny planned to kill him on his return that night. Fortunately, one of Owiny's wives who knew of the plan did not approve of the idea. So she watched for Okuro's return and when she saw him at a distance, she slipped out of the home and went to meet him where no one could see them.

She asked Okuro for one guinea fowl, and he being naturally kind-hearted, gave it to her without any hesitation. The woman then told him of the secret and advised him to leave as soon as he could.

Okuro thanked her and secretly collected what he could and left that night back to Gafumbulire. He passed through areas infested with elephants and lions, but he finally arrived safely.

He later moved to near River Sio where he lived and bore five children: Okumu, Oseno, Sigulu, Adera and Siganda. They are the forefathers of the Abakhulo. Chief Ngira, whom the first Europeans found in Bukhekhe, was a great-grandson of Oseno.

6. MAREEBA OF MARACH

Mareeba was the founder of the Abafofoyo of Marach. His father was a man called Khayanga, and his mother was Naliali. It is said that Mareeba had two brothers, Were Khaayo, who is the founder of the Abaguuri clan in Bukhayo, and Owiny Sigoma, who later joined the Luos and became a leader among them.

Mareeba used to live in the home of his forefathers in Ibanda on the Uganda side of Berkeley Bay. His home was at a place called Lugala. When he separated with Owiny and Were Khaayo, he went to Rukala in Bunyala (Busia District). He moved through various places till he finally came to Marach. His forefathers were famous rainmakers and he himself became a rainmaker and consequently a chief in Marach.

Mareeba had several sons: Omoto, Mukamwanja, Nambanja, Puapu (or Piapu), Mufutu, Ngusa and Musundi. He employed many Masai warriors to raid cattle for him. It is said that when he died he bequeathed his throne to Mukamwanja, but the Masai deposed him and put the youngest son on the throne. The result was a family war, and some of Mareeba's sons to avoid trouble fled to other places where they have founded branches of the Abofofoyo clan. For instance, Nambanja fled and founded the Abafofoyo of Siongo in Bukhekhe.

7. SAYWA OF BUNYALA BUONGO

The ancestors of Saywa, the Abamulembo, came from Tiriki from a group of people known as Abarwa (or Abatwa). They next went to Wanga (Emanga) from where they moved on through Uholo to Marach.

Saywa was the son of Murwa, who had taught him the family trade of blacksmithing. While in Marach Saywa became very famous as a blacksmith. One day the Masai (Abaseebe) came to him and handed him a human skull, saying that if he was as good as his fame, he should be able to forge the skull into a spear. Saywa knew that they were only seeking for an excuse to kill him. So he told them to wait while he went to fetch some implements. At this opportunity he hurried to his brother's house and told him of his trouble. His brother advised him to take little pieces of iron and place them secretly in the sockets of the skull. Saywa went back and told the Abeseebe to come back the following day when he would forge the spear in their presence.

While they were away he put the pieces of iron in the sockets, and next day he apparently forged the skull into a spear, much to the amazement of the Abaseebe. They were so impressed that they gave him a bull.

About this time the chief of Marach, Mareeba, died and for fear of a possible civil war, Saywa moved away from Marach with Mareeba's younger son, Nambanja. Unfortunately, Saywa's bull was so fierce that it gored and killed local bulls wherever Saywa went; and the people insisted that he must either kill it or leave the area. He did not kill it. So they moved from place to place. Finally they got to Siongo in Bukhekhe. Nambanja remained here, but Saywa had to keep moving, first to Ibanda, then to Sigulu Island, then to Runyu in Bunyala, and finally to Buongo in present-day Bunyala.

At Buongo he found that it had not rained for a long time and the people ate only pumpkins. He told them that he could cause rain to fall. They said that if he did so they would make him their chief. So he went back to his friends, the Abafofoyo, and got them to give him the power to make rain. When he got back to Buongo, it rained heavily for several days. The people had a large harvest that year. So they made Saywa their chief, and his descendants have been chiefs in Bunyala ever since. His three sons, Lwang'a, Pondi and Kwambo are the founders of the three major sub-clans of the Abamulembo clan. The ruling powers were handed down to the youngest son, Kwambo.

Chapter 8

Great Tribal Leaders of Buluyia

1. WANGA

The founder of the Abawanga sub-tribe was a man called Wanga. He lived in Tiriki near Kaimosi, where his ancestors had come after leaving the area of the lake.

His father, Muwanga, decided that Wanga should inherit his chieftainship, even though he was not the eldest son. This annoyed Wanga's elder brothers, and they hated him. This was made worse when Wanga's wife proved to be a thief. When she stole the bananas of Wanga's brother, Khabiakala, the latter made the matter public, and Wanga was so ashamed that he disappeared from the home, and no one could guess where he had gone.

He moved on to Emaanga, which today is between Mumias and Musanda. There he found the following clans: Abamwima, Abamanga, and Abamulembwa. A member of the Abamwima called Liyai was the chief there. Wanga went to Liyai's home and pretended to be a very poor man. He asked for menial work, to clean the stables and the kraal.

He did this work for about two weeks. He only worked with one hand, keeping the other one in the pocket of his skin dress. All the people in Liyai's home thought that he was lame, except one of the chief's wives who did not trust the intentions of Wanga.

One day, after taking him food in the stable, she pretended to be going away, but then went quietly behind the stable and looked through an opening in the wall. She saw just what she had been suspecting: Wanga had taken out his hidden hand and on it was a royal ring (*omukasa*).

She went and told Liyai about it. Liyai called Wanga and reprimanded him for doing such a thing. 'You have ruined my family', he said. It was a custom that, if a man made another royal person do menial work, ill luck would come to him who was worked for.

After talking over the whole problem, Liyai suggested that he should kill a sheep and brew beer and make a special feast to take away the curse. Wanga agreed.

On the day of the feast, five strangers appeared in Liyali's home, among the crowd. They were Wanga's servants who had come from Tiriki in search of their master.

After the feast the five servants went back with Wanga to Tiriki. The five were the ancestors of the following clans: Abashikawa, Abakalibo, Ababuka, Abachero and Abakhami.

Later, Wanga left Kaimosi with the whole of his family and his servants and settled in Emaanga. And, as Liyai had feared, he finally got rid of the Abamwima and became the ruler of the country and gave it his name, Wanga.

2. MUBUKUSU

Mubukusu used to live with his father and his mother near Mbale in Uganda. His father was called Maina; his brothers were Chesekweli, Msaaba and Kimalemi.

One day Chesekweli (Mubukusu's eldest brother) committed a bad crime with his father's younger wife. His father, Maina, was very angry with him. He called together all his sons and his Teso neighbours and told them that he was going to kill Chesekweli because of the crime.

Some of Maina's children agreed to this. The Teso neighbours also agreed that Chesekweli should die. But Mubukusu objected. He said that, although the crime was a very bad one, it did not deserve death.

This annoyed his father so much that Mubukusu was ordered to leave Maina's home immediately, together with Chesekweli and their families, and anybody else who sympathized with them.

That is how the Babukusu (descendants of Mubukusu) separated from Bagisu, who descend from Masaaba.

Mubukusu and Chesekweli and all their families and followers left Mbale and settled at Tororo, which was then called Bubuya. Chesekweli and others later moved on to Shukulu hills nearby, which was then called Buyemba.

After some time the Teso followed them there and began to chase them into Kenya. The followers of Mubukusu camped at Amukura. But the Teso followed them there too and drove them away. When Mubukusu died, his son, Mango, took over the leadership of the group. It is said that the Teso chased the Babukusu until, over many years, they rounded Mt. Elgon (Masaaba) three times. When the Babukusu became numerous enough to resist the Teso, they settled in the Malawisi area, and the Teso settled to the west of them where they are still living today.

3. NETIA WAMUKOYA

One of the most powerful kings (*Nabongo*) of Wanga was called Netia Wamukoya, often simply called Netia. He was a tall cruel man who was dreaded both by his subjects and by his enemies.

Netia employed large groups of Masai (Abakwabi) warriors who raided the neighbouring tribes and brought the cattle and women to Netia at Lureko, near Mumias. Netia then gave them some of the cattle to keep as pay.

Netia was fond of making beer parties. To these parties he would invite neighbours, including some of the Masai. In every one of these parties someone died, and Netia always suggested that the dead one had over-drunk or over-eaten.

At first the Masai used to accept this explanation, but later they began to suspect Netia.

One day they decided to look out for any tricks that Netia or anybody else might play at the party. They knew that the ones who died always sat at a special place in the beer hall.

The drinking went on for a long time. Then, when Netia thought that they were drunk, he slipped the loop of a rope round the neck of the man who was sitting at the usual place. The length of the rope was passed through a round hole in the wall, and as a servant outside the room prepared to pull it and so strangle the man, the watchful Masai jumped up and caused a row. They tried to get hold of Netia, but he escaped and hid himself near River Nzoia.

The Masai searched for him angrily for several days. Finally they found him and speared him to death. Thus ended the reign of one of the most powerful rulers of the Wanga Empire. His son, Osundwa, succeeded him. Osundwa was the great-grandfather of Mumia.

4. THE GREAT MUMIA

Mumia was born around 1850. His father was Shiundu, a great-grandson of Netia. Mumia's mother gave birth to many children, but all of them died. So when she gave birth to this last child, she called him Makokha according to Luyia custom. She also placed him on the path so that the child might be picked up by a stranger. All this was supposed to ensure that the child would not die like the other children of his mother.

The little boy Makokha was born during a war between the Teso (Abamia) and the Waholo to the south of South Wanga. So the child was named Omumia in memory of that war. This name stuck, and when he grew up and succeeded his father in 1881 or 1882 as Nabongo, everybody knew him as Mumia.

Mumia was a tall, slender, slow-moving man who ate only a little special food daily; by custom he was not supposed to eat most of the food that ordinary people eat. He was a very wise man and his judgements were respected by everybody.

When the first Europeans arrived in this country, they passed through his home and he gave them much help. Also, when the Europeans established their government in this country, he co-operated with them. He sent Wanga chiefs to different parts of Buluyia to establish the new government there.

In 1909 he was made paramount chief, which means that all the other chiefs in the area had to recognize him as chief over them.

Mumia was retired from the office of paramount chief in 1926; but a new paramount chief was not appointed.

He had nearly 100 wives, and many more children.

He died in April, 1949, aged about a hundred years.

5. CHIEF NDOMBI

Ndombi was the son of Mayero of the Abayirifuma clan. He became the first chief of the Banyala of Kakamega District soon after the arrival of the Europeans.

First, as a young man he led the Abanyala in a war against the early British administration. Later, Mumia appointed him chief of the Abanyala. The Banyala had been hiding in the nearby forest, which they called *ulukaka lwa Mayero*, and Ndombi persuaded them to come out of it after he became chief.

Ndombi was an able and powerful ruler, but he was unfortunately not a kind man. He made the Abanyala work all day and severely punished those who were either lazy or who disobeyed his orders. Whenever he visited any place, he expected the people to bring to him many presents of food and domestic animals which were then taken to his many wives. In this way he became very rich.

During his rule the Banyala grew a lot of food under his orders; but at the same time he made many of them work for him without pay.

He died in 1940.

Chapter 9

Some Unusual People

1. WACHIYE WA NAUMBWA

Wachiye lived in Bukusu and he was of the Abakitwika clan (Abakwanga sub-clan). There are many stories told about him. He is supposed to have worked many miraculous deeds, such as walking on water, lighting a fire on top of water and cooking on it, lighting a fire on a grass roof without burning the house, and so on.

His leadership was recognized throughout Bukusu and there were regular meetings at his home. During the meetings he used to sit on a spear point instead of on a stool.

He was very brave in battle and often fought a battle single-handed, without needing any helpers.

It is said that through the years he did not get old. Further, the Babukusu say he did not die; he simply disappeared with his wife and is still living somewhere in hiding. He will one day come back!

2. SUMBA

Sumba lived many years ago on the two islands of Sigulu and Sumba in Berkeley Bay (Lake Victoria). The full story of his life is kept secret by those of his clan (Abakhabotsa), but he is believed to have performed miracles, and when he died, a religious festival with dancing, wrestling, sacrifices and feasting was established annually. This used to be held on Sumba Island and people came from long distances to attend.

Then some generations later a girl of his family got married to a boy of the Abakhoone clan in western Bunyala near Port Victoria. After some years of marriage, it is said that the spirit of Sumba followed her and entered her. It told her that the Sumba Annual Festival should henceforth be organized by her offspring.

That is how the Sumba festival was moved from the islands and from its organizers, the Abakhabotsa, to western Bunyala among the Abakhoone, who still organize it to the present day.

The festival used to be a great occasion, and people used to come from as far away as Samia and Alego to attend it. It lasted several days during which the special festival drums were beating continuously, with the women dancing to them. During the day there was a wrestling contest which made the Abanyala very famous wrestlers.

There were many important restrictions during the Sumba Festival. For instance, immorality of any kind or fighting was punishable by natural death unless purified by special sacrifice. Also heavy fines were imposed.

The food and beer required at the festival was collected from the whole of Bunyala as a matter of custom. No one could refuse to contribute and if he did it was believed there would be no rain, and no one wanted to be blamed for this. So about two months before the festival the organizers went round the country beating their drum and collecting the grain and chickens.

The early missionaries thought the practice was evil and forbade the Christians to go to the festival or contribute to it. Later they found that there was nothing wrong with attending the day ceremonies.

3. NAKHABUKA

Nakhabuka was a girl of the Abamakhya clan in Bunyala. She lived during the last century, a bit more than a hundred years ago. She was believed to be the most beautiful girl in the country. The fame of her beauty went far and wide. She is also said to have been a girl of very clean habits, and a virgin.

A group of the Abasamia (of the Abakokho clan) heard about her and came to abduct her and marry her. They found her at a place called Burangasi near Makunda Intermediate School. She was bathing on the banks of River Nzoia. She refused their approaches and one of them shot her with an arrow; then they ran away. She struggled home with the arrow in her body, and the blood dripping. When she reached near her home, she fell down and died.

It is said that a fig tree grew in every place where her blood dropped; and very many fig trees grew near the place where she fell and died. They are still there to the present day. And in the nearby plain of Bukhwanga an annual festival has been held with wrestling, etc. (identical with the Sumba Festival) up to the present day.

4. OTIENO

Otieno did not perform miracles like the three people we have seen above. He fought against slave traders and freed the slaves they were taking away. He lived at Bumaba near the mouth of River Nzoia.

He was a tall, brave man who smoked opium to make him fearless. He organized a large group of brave men to capture the canoes of slave traders coming from Uganda to collect slaves and ferry them back to Busoga in Uganda. The slave traders used to row their canoes to a convenient landing and, when curious and unsuspecting villagers came to look at them, the slavers jumped at them and captured them. Then they tied them and took them away in their boats.

When the practice began to increase, Otieno organized his group. He got together many large canoes to be used for chasing the slave traders. He made special spears, each with a long string attached to it, so that after spearing an enemy the spear could be pulled back, and also because the pulling could rock the boat of the enemy and overturn it.

Otieno had a sentry who sat in a tall tree which still stands alone near the mouth of River Nzoia. As soon as the sentry noticed the enemies' canoes approaching from a long distance, he alerted Otieno's men and they put away their opium pipes and got into their special canoes. Then they dashed openly for the enemy. As soon as they got within a reasonable distance, they released their spears towards the nearest enemy canoe. The spears which did not strike anything were quickly pulled back. If any of the spears stuck into a person or the canoe, it was pulled in such a way as to overturn the enemy canoe.

In this way Otieno killed many slave traders, and in the end succeeded in discouraging others from coming. In this way he helped to bring that evil trade to an end.

Otieno lived in the second half of the last century.

Chapter 10

Stories of Tribal Warfare

1. PREPARATION FOR WAR

Warriors usually were between the ages of 18 and 40. There were rules that all warriors had to observe, especially when preparing for war. For instance, in some places they were not to associate with women at such a time. They had to know how to handle the various weapons they were to use. They had to know how to hold the shield in various positions to defend themselves against the enemies' spears.

In some sub-tribes, young men of between 18 and 21 were taken to camp for some weeks in a year and trained in the various rules and techniques of war. Here, in addition to the general rules of warfare, they would learn that women were not to be speared in a war. Other persons that were not to be killed were: a messenger of an enemy tribe who came to announce a war; or a messenger of an enemy tribe who came to announce the surrender of his tribe.

The captives of war were taken and were usually made slaves. The men had to become *abasumba* to work for their master. In time, if they were good, they would be given a plot of land and maybe a wife too, so as to make their own homes. Captured children were made to grow up as members of the new tribe, though they kept their clan names. Girls and women were often married without any bride price.

Many Baluyia villages were protected either by a wall, or by a ditch (*olukoba*), or both. These went all round the village, and were useful in resisting raiders who came at night: these raiders were mostly Nandi, Masai and Teso.

2. WARRIORS' DRESS AND WEAPONS

When going to war, the warriors usually painted themselves so as to look as frightening as possible. Some wore horns on their heads, and also feathers.

The weapons consisted of spears and special javelins. Sometimes these were attached to a long string so that, after spearing an enemy, the spear could be pulled back again and used once more.

A fight with spears required shields for protection. These were cleverly made out of the hides of certain animals, notably the buffalo. At the back of the shield was often painted the symbol of the clan of the warrior.

Arrows were also used, especially by sub-tribes neighbouring the Nandi or Masai.

Swords and special knives, as well as clubs, were also used.

3. LOCAL WARFARE

Tribal wars were fought only locally. That is, often a clan fought a neighbouring enemy clan, or a tribe fought a neighbouring enemy tribe. Usually the war did not spread very far, and some wars consisted only of one battle. A few wars, however, were big and spread to other places, thus involving many people. An example of this is the war of 'Eshiatikho' which will be described below.

Many of the tribal wars in Buluyia were caused by cattle raids from neighbouring non-Luyia tribes. The Teso fought many wars against the Babukusu and the Bakhayo and even penetrated into Samia. The Luos fought wars against the Baluyia groups neighbouring them, for instance, near Maseno and Luanda, near Musanda, and in Usonga.

The Nandi fought the Baluyia in Kabras, Isukha and Tiriki; while the Masai of Uasin Gishu used to make regular raids on the Baluyia for looting cattle.

Local wars within Buluyia were mainly caused when the young men of a tribe or a clan kidnapped a girl of another clan or tribe; or when they killed a member of another clan or tribe who was passing through their territory.

4. A STORY OF TRIBAL WARFARE

The war story told below is of special interest to all Baluyia because it led to great changes in the arrangement of clans and sub-tribes in Buluyia. It is known as the war of 'Ifunikho' in some places and as the war of 'Eshiatikho' in others, notably in Kabras and Bunyala in the Kakamega District.

The War of 'Eshiatikho': This war occurred in Bunyala in the Busia District, near Lake Victoria, between the Rivers Nzoia and Yala.

It was really a war waged by all the clans of the area against the Abakhoone, a powerful clan which lived close to the mouth of River Yala called Ndekwe. The Abakhoone had fought and expelled many clans from nearby. These clans had to leave the area and cross River Sio to the area of Busia in Uganda. Others had to go to Luo country. Those who remained near the Abakhoone continually suffered from the cruelties of this clan.

So, around 1800 they organized themselves against the clan. The following clans took an active part in getting rid of Abakhoone: Abalwani, Abamatseke, Ababboro, Abang'oma, Abamulembo, Abamakhya, Abanyifwa, Abanyekera, Abasinyama, Abayineki and Abakhumatsi.

They knew that singly they were not able to defeat the fierce Abakhoone. So they held a war council. The war council decided to fetch a medicineman from Mfwang'ano Island in Lake Victoria. A member of the Abalwani clan, whose name was Simwero, was the one who went to fetch him. He was eager to do this job because his brother, called Obwori, had been cruelly murdered by the Abakhoone, who had removed a rib from him and left him to die in pain. This was their popular way of killing people in peace time.

The medicine-man came at last. His medicine was called *omusala kwe ifulu* (the medicine of the little fish). Simwero brought him to a place called E Sigomere in the home of Abamatseke clan. There he performed his witchcraft. He killed a goat which had drunk medicine, and its carcass was placed secretly in the *olukoba* (ditch) of the Abakhoone near a place called Syanzofwe.

The Abakhoone picked up the animal and ate it in merriment; which was all according to plan. Within a day, all those Abakhoone who had eaten of the dead animal fell sick, and the other clans declared war upon them.

Now the Abakhoone had many famous warriors. There was Mufuula, the one-eyed general of their army. There was Esakha, the fastest runner of them all. There was Matsaba, and there were many others. The Abakhoone knew that as long as these brave soldiers were alive, no clan or combination of clans would defeat them.

The first battle of this war was fought in Syanzofwe, which is a flat, open space near the southern bank of River Nzoia and about two miles from its mouth.

None of the veteran warriors of the Abakhoone went to this battle. They left the younger men to fight the weak clans which they had learnt to despise. They themselves remained home to bury their dead, who had died so mysteriously.

That first battle was a victory for the united clans. They were led by a brave warrior called Makanda of the Abamulembo clan, a brother of the chief of the united clans. Makanda and his army were ruthless and determined, and the Abakhoone had to retreat in confusion.

This was the first defeat the Abakhoone had suffered for many, many generations, and it was a great shock to them. In the next battle Matsaba was sent to lead their army. But it was all in vain. Nearly the whole battalion was wiped out, and Matsaba himself was killed.

The Abakhoone now realized that the war was a serious matter, and that they were in danger of being defeated. They sent a greater force to the next battle, but that too was wiped out. So in the following battle Mufuula himself had to lead the Abakhoone army, assisted by Esakha.

As soon as the battle started, Mufuula was speared to death, and Esakha and the rest of the army fled in confusion, to hide in the Yala swamp with their frightened families. There they were pursued and many were speared like animals. They were hunted throughout the night. Some had been foolish enough to flee with their hens and cocks. Their whereabouts were found when the cocks began to crow, and they were attacked and killed. The survivors do not eat a chicken, wherever they are found, to the present day. The whereabouts of the others was known when the little bells (*tsindeke*) on the children's wrists and ankles sounded. This has led to some groups of Abakhoone holding *indeke* as taboo.

Those who managed to escape fled to far-off places—Bukusu (where you find Namajanja's family), Bukhayo, Samia-Bugwe in Uganda, Bunyuli in Uganda, and Mfwang'ano Island in Lake Victoria. As they moved, other clans had to flee too, ahead of them; and a rearrangement of clans resulted in the whole of Buluyia.

5. THE WAR OF CHETAMBE

When the British began to introduce their government in this country, they received much resistance from some of the tribes. Those who resisted most were the Babukusu. Between 1894 and 1898 they caused much trouble against the Sudanese soldiers of the British. The most memorable of these battles was fought at Chetambe's fort, near Broderick Falls. Actually, Chetambe's fort belonged to the Tachon, but the Babukusu entered it while escaping.

The government collected together a large army consisting of Sudanese troops, many Masai warriors, and one thousand Baganda soldiers led by the famous Kakungulu.

The large army marched from South Bukusu towards Bungoma, shooting and frightening people. By the time the troops reached Bungoma, the Babukusu were so frightened that they fled desperately towards the east, across the plain between Bungoma and Broderick Falls. The government forces raced after them. Many women and children could not keep up the fast pace and gave up running away altogether. Some of them were shot by the passing troops.

When the first Babukusu reached Chetambe's fort, the Tachoni owners of it had run away to hide in the forests to the east. So the Babukusu entered the fort. When the government forces arrived, there were several thousand Babukusu men, women and children in the fort. The government forces shot at the fort for many hours. In the end they jumped over the low wall facing the east and shot everyone they found still alive inside.

So many people were killed that the rest of the Babukusu gave up the resistance against the British.

The Babukusu composed a song about the battle of Chetambe: '*Khwafwa Khwabuna eee nga lumerera, wa Chetambe eee nga lumerera eee.*'

Chapter 11

Marriage Among the Baluyia

1. HOW MARRIAGE WAS ARRANGED

This was done in one of two ways. In one case the father of a boy arranged with the father of a girl with or without the knowledge of the boy. In the other case, the boy himself looked for a hard-working girl from a reputed family. He was usually accompanied by his boy friends. The meeting place was usually in or near the girl's home. She too came to the meeting place accompanied by her girl friends. The question was then put to the girl, and if she agreed, both parties went to tell their parents.

Before the boy or his father approached to make the suggestion, careful, private inquiries were made about the girl's character and her ability to work. A go-between (*wangira*) was often used.

Before accepting—sometimes even after accepting—the girl too caused inquiries to be made about the boy's character. She also scrutinized his deformities, if any.

When everything was checked, male relatives of the boy visited the girl's parents to talk things over, and if necessary, start paying the dowry.

In some parts of Buluyia the boy gave the girl a token (e.g. *eshitiiri*, a bangle) to indicate that they were now engaged.

2. PAYING THE DOWRY (OKHUKHWA)

This differed slightly from place to place. Generally, it was done in instalments. Representatives of the boy took the items available to the girl's home where they met her parents and relatives. Usually a beer party was made for the meeting. During the party important matters concerning the dowry would be discussed.

The items of dowry were cows and bulls. The equivalent of a cow was four goats, and of a bull, three goats, depending on local practice. The equivalent of a goat was, on the average, three hoes. (In some places it was an insult to pay a sheep as dowry.)

Every time an item was brought equivalent to a cow or bull, a short stick was cut and marked and then tied on the little bundle of similar sticks denoting earlier instalments. The girl's parents kept one bundle; the boy's parents went away with another for the record. These bundles had to be kept carefully in case some of the animals died and had to be returned to the boy's home, as happened in some places; they were also kept in case the marriage did not materialize, or would end up in a divorce, in which cases some of the items had to be refunded.

The final amount or total paid again depended on local custom. In some places three to six head of cattle or their equivalent were sufficient. In other places it was more (sometimes much more), say between thirteen and twenty head of cattle.

In other places there was an initial number of cattle to be paid in; the number depended on the bargaining power of both parties. The second lot of cattle was 'customary' and had to be paid, thus precluding bargaining. This practice was commonest in western Buluyia. There, four head of cattle had to be paid: a cow for the mother, a cow for the father (paternal uncle), a bull or cow for the maternal uncle, and a bull for the brother (usually paternal cousin).

When these were paid, there remained many small but important items which were paid to the girl or her relatives during or shortly after the marriage feast.

Note: Certain relatives of the boy helped to subscribe the items for the dowry. Certain relatives of the girl got a share of the dowry.

3. THE MARRIAGE FEAST (SHITIALO)

When the parents and relatives of the girl were satisfied with the dowry paid, arrangements were made for the wedding. (Note: There were only a few cases where the dowry was satisfactory to the parents. It was only in such cases that the type of wedding described here took place.)

A big feast was prepared, both at the girl's home and at the boy's home. The boy, together with his friends, went to the girl's home to fetch her. There was much singing at the girl's home. When everything was ready, the boys left with the bride and a large group of girls to act as bridesmaids. These girls sang wedding songs the whole way to the boy's home. (Note: In some places the boy had to go and live at the girl's home cultivating, fetching water and fetching firewood, to prove that he was suitable as a hardworking husband. This was done before *Eshitialo*.)

In some cases the boy did not come to fetch his bride in the manner explained. Instead, the girl's brothers and male cousins accompanied her and her bridesmaids to the groom's home.

At the groom's home, too, the women of his side sang appropriate songs. There was much dancing, drinking and eating.

As soon as the bride entered the home, certain customs were observed. These differed slightly from place to place. In some areas the girl ate only food from her home or her relatives until the customary fees for eating the boy's food were paid.

After the first night there were several things to be done, and again they varied from place to place. If the girl was found a virgin, there was a great deal of festivity and dancing, and presents for her mother.

During one of the days of the marriage feast (for it sometimes lasted several days), certain animals were killed to fulfil various customs. The meat was also shared according to custom, which also differed from place to place.

Note: Where the dowry was not sufficient, the girl had to be dragged by men hired by the boy. There was usually a fight with the girl's male relatives, and if the opposition was strong some people were badly hurt.

4. THE MARRIAGE CEREMONY

This was called *Eshitishio* in some places. It consisted in the killing of a cow (in other places a he-goat) to fulfil a custom; the meat was shared and cooked according to custom. It was usually the climax of the marriage ceremony. Where a girl had to receive a fee in order to start eating the boy's food, she received it on this day.

A kind of ceremony was carried out in the boy's mother's hut; the bride entered this hut for the first time during the ceremony. Several customary presents were given to the girl for the various functions she was going to perform: cooking, fetching firewood, fetching water, etc. This practice varied according to locality.

Note: The marriage ceremonies in Maragoli, Tiriki, Idakho and Isukha are in some details very different from the practice elsewhere in Buluyia.

5. TYPES OF MARRIAGES

There were several. The most perfect was the one described above. There was also marriage by elopement when the girl and the boy agreed to marry without their parents' consent. There was marriage by forceful dragging of a girl for whom no dowry or very little had previously been paid. In either case there was a definite procedure later to make the marriage valid; and dowry had to be paid sooner or later.

In western Buluyia only, a man married his older brother's wife when the brother died. Where there was no younger brother to inherit the wife according to custom, a male cousin took her instead. This type of marriage was called *okhukerama*; it was not practised among some eastern Baluyia.

The opposite type of marriage was when a man married the sister or female cousin of his wife—while the wife was still alive or after she was dead. This marriage was called *eshibeyo* and again it was practised mainly among the western Baluyia.

Chapter 12

Tribal Government in Old Times

1. THE OLUKONGO AS A UNIT

The smallest unit of government was the *olukongo,* consisting of several villages situated on a ridge or in a valley. The *olukongo* had a leader who usually acted as chairman in the council of elders of the *olukongo.* He was consulted on all important matters, but usually he only issued orders when together with the council, not on his own.

2. WHAT MADE A MAN A LEADER

The leader of *olukongo* was generally the chief landowner of that area. Where there was no able leader among the landowners, then the local rainmaker was the accepted leader. Where there was no such, then the chief medicine-man acted as chief. In other words, the accepted chief of *olukongo* was a man who was able to wield a great deal of influence over the people in his area. In many cases this leadership was handed down from father to son within one clan, and other clans were afraid of usurping the function in case the rain should stop coming and they would be blamed for it.

3. THE COUNCIL OF ELDERS

The leader had a group of advisers raised from local clans. These formed the inner council. But there was in many places a kind of open *baraza* where everyone could come to listen and where all adult men could speak. This open council provided an opportunity for everyone to air their views, but the real decisions were taken by the inner council in private. They, of course, took into account the decisions of the open council, and often merely confirmed them.

In important matters such as that of declaring war, the inner council discussed the matter and then brought it before the open council, which usually went by the speech of the spokesman of the inner council.

Ordinary cases between citizens were first discussed openly in the open council and then finalized in the inner council.

In some places there was also a bigger council consisting of several *tsingongo*. In Wanga there was the biggest council of all (a tribal council) to advise the Nabongo.

The council of *olukongo* also decided or helped to decide when the periods of cultivation, etc., should start. It arranged for the local annual festival of sports and dances; it summoned warriors and fetched the rainmaker.

4. HOW THEY KEPT LAW AND ORDER

The censure or blame by the open council was feared and respected. People dreaded appearing before the public on a shameful matter. Hence there were very few serious crimes committed. As a result, the usual crimes consisted of debts of property or of dowry, or land cases. Theft, murder or sexual crimes were frowned upon and anyone accused of them was despised and avoided for life.

Everyone in the *olukongo* was known and so when he was wanted at the council he had to come. This made the work of keeping order easy. Also, people readily came to give evidence, even against their own relatives, especially where serious or shameful crimes were involved.

5. HOW CASES WERE TRIED

As it has been stated, cases between citizens were first brought before the open council. It did not take much time before people realized who was telling the truth.

In the judgement of simple cases, the elders simply asked both the accused and the accuser to seek peace between each other.

In cases where compensation was necessary, the elders ensured that it was paid. In serious cases, e.g. murder, a whole clan had to help its member to pay a large number of cattle. In a case of rape, cattle were also paid. In cases of theft, heavy penalties had to be paid and the criminal had in addition to be ostracized.

In cases where the accused completely denied the charges, the elders resorted to a practice known as *eshilulu*. The accused was asked to carry or jump over the *eshilulu* to prove that what he was saying was true and that he was not guilty. This was the most important form of swearing in Buluyia. No one dared undergo it unless he was certain he was innocent, because, if he was not, the *eshilulu* was supposed to kill him sooner or later. The *eshilulu* was usually resorted to in cases of serious theft or witchcraft.

When a boy made a girl pregnant and denied it, he was made to pass between the legs of the girl. If he was guilty, the action would kill him. If the girl was telling a lie, she would suffer similar consequences. Some old women were expert at telling who the father of an illegitimate child was soon after birth; and so, very often, a case of pregnancy waited till the baby was born.

Offences against people's daughters or wives were punishable in the form of a fine in cattle.

Hurting anyone in a fight or otherwise was also punishable by a similar fine.

There were no prisons. But in serious cases where a person had to be ostracized, it was a worse penalty than a prison sentence: sometimes it affected not only the person, but his children as well. Among the Baluyia, loss of reputation was a serious matter.

6. TYPES OF CASES

The commonest cases were those concerning land. But witchcraft or suspected witchcraft was not uncommon. This was punished by ostracism or by beating to death. A medicine-man was not considered a witch; but one who was supposed to cause stomach-ache in children or adults, or to cause sickness or death by magic, was considered a witch and a criminal.

Marriage irregularities were another common case. For instance, abduction of a girl for marriage without paying any or sufficient dowry; forgetting to complete the instalments which were deferred; a woman running away from her husband. Adultery, rape and similar offences were very, very rare.

Theft was also a common type of case. Theft of cattle was especially common, but it usually concerned people of different *tsingongo* or clans or tribes, and it was usually settled by the elders of both parties getting together and deciding on the compensation.

Refusal to co-operate in a communal effort, e.g. building a walled village, going to a hunt or to a war, would also be brought before an open council and often resulted in ostracism.

The rest of the cases concerned irregularities about local customs. If one was found to violate a custom or to have desecrated a holy place (*eshiyembekho*), then a sacrifice of a chicken or goat was performed to remove the curse.

7. TAXES

There were no formal taxes. But whenever payment was required for anything, the inner council authorized collection of the grain, chickens or cattle required.

Such payment would be needed to pay for a case of murder or a man killed in war; the fees of a rainmaker; contribution to an annual festival in the form of food; contribution for feeding a large group of visitors; presents for the chief or local leader on certain occasions, and so on.

Chapter 13

Local Government Today

1. THE NEW LEADERS

Nowadays in place of the tribal council of elders there is the Location Council of elected representatives. Each location is ruled by a chief. Under the chief are the sub-chiefs ruling sub-locations. Under these there are the *milangos*, each heading the *olukongo*. Under the *milangos* are the village leaders (sometimes called *kujeje*). An important function of the chief and those under him is to collect taxes and rates.

2. LOCATION COUNCILS

There are the following Location Councils in Buluyia:

Kakamega District: East Bunyore, West Bunyore, South Maragoli, North Maragoli, Tiriki, Idakho, Isukha, Kabras, Bunyala, Butsotso, Kisa and Marama.

Bungoma District: South Bukusu, East Bukusu, Ndibisi, Bokoli, Elgon, Malakisi and Kimilili.

Busia District: North Teso, South Teso, Bukhayo, Marach, Samia and Bunyala.

3. BIGGER LOCAL COUNCILS

Above the Location Council is the County Council, which also consists of representatives elected by the people. There are three County Councils in Buluyia: Kakamega County Council, Bungoma County Council and Busia County Council.

Each County Council has committees to cater for the various services for which the council is responsible; e.g. Law and Order, Finance, Health, Education, Agriculture, Roads, Trade and Markets, etc.

The County Council covers the area of a district. At the top of the administration of a district is the District Commissioner. He is assisted by the Assistant District Commissioner, the District Officers, and the District Assistants, as well as district agricultural, education, etc., officers.

The County Council passes by-laws for the county.

4. The Province

The biggest local governing body is the province. Buluyia consists of one province called the Western Province. It has a Provincial Advisory Council of 27 elected representatives. There are also four specially elected members. The Council has a Chairman and Vice-Chairman.

The actual administration of the province is headed by the Provincial Commissioner. The Provincial Advisory Council also has committees to cater for its services. It has powers to make by-laws on certain subjects for the good of the province.

There are seven provinces in the whole of Kenya. Nairobi is extra, and is the capital of our country. The Government has decided that the Provincial Advisory Councils should continue in existence until the next general elections, by which time measures will have been taken to dissolve them. Meanwhile the councils may hold four sessions a year, each not lasting more than three days. Members of the Provincial Advisory Councils receive salaries and sitting allowances.

5. The Rates and their Collection

Nowadays people pay a graduated personal tax to their County Council which is collected by the administration. Under this new system, the lowest tax is 48/- for people earning little money. Those earning high incomes pay more, according to the amount they earn per year. The highest tax under this system is 600/- for those earning above £600 per year. It is the government's policy progressively to exempt from this direct tax people earning extremely low incomes.

These taxes help to pay for local services such as health, roads, education, agriculture, markets, and so on.

Other revenue is obtained from licences (e.g. of bicycles, or beer halls) and in subventions from the government.

Note: The Western Province consists of the Abaluyia plus the Teso and the Elkony, who live on the slopes of Mt. Elgon.

Chapter 14

Shelters of Long Ago

1. TYPES OF DWELLINGS AND THEIR CONSTRUCTION

The standard hut in Buluyia was made of sticks filled in and plastered with mud. The roof structure was tied with sticks and was thatched with grass or local reeds. The floor was beaten hard and then regularly smeared with cowdung.

There was only one door in the common hut. There were no windows, but openings were left all round the top of the wall for ventilation. Often little round holes were also left in the wall to let in fresh air.

The roof provided wide eaves to make a verandah. Parts of the verandah had a wall round them to be used as a store for firewood, and also to house

GROUND PLAN OF A LUYIA HUT

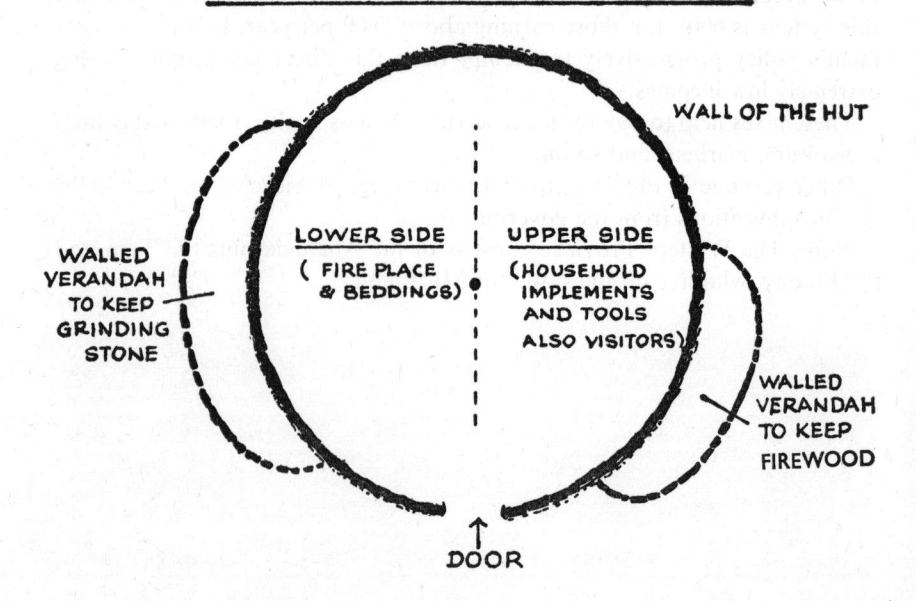

- WALL OF THE HUT
- WALLED VERANDAH TO KEEP GRINDING STONE
- LOWER SIDE (FIRE PLACE & BEDDINGS)
- UPPER SIDE (HOUSEHOLD IMPLEMENTS AND TOOLS ALSO VISITORS)
- WALLED VERANDAH TO KEEP FIREWOOD
- DOOR

the grinding stone (*oluchina*).

Before a new hut could be erected, the father or uncle of the owner had to be present to place the first stick in the ground. If the place was away from any old home, that is, if it was *olukala*, a chicken had to be killed and a little ceremony performed.

On some occasions a very temporary hut built with sticks and grass only was erected for the inmates. This was necessary when starting a new home, or during certain types of funerals, or for people isolated due to an infectious disease such as leprosy.

An unmarried man's hut was called *isimba*, and an old woman's hut where girls slept was called *eshibinzie*. The latter was also called *isimba* in Bukusu.

2. LAYOUT OF HOMES AND HUTS

There was a definite arrangement of huts in the home. This differed slightly from place to place. The usual order was as follows: the hut of the first wife was directly opposite the gate of the home. That of the second wife was to the right of it; that of the third to the left of it, and so on alternately till all the huts of the wives were placed. The oldest son's hut (*isimba*) was nearer the gate and to the right as you stand facing the gate. The second son's hut was at a corresponding place to the left; the third son's followed the first's on the gate side, and so on until all the sons' huts were provided for. Slaves or adopted strangers who were allowed to build a hut in the home were given the place of the youngest son.

The stable for goats or kraal for cattle was in the centre of the circle of huts. If the man had a special hut, without a wife in it, it was also near the centre of the home.

The arrangement of the furniture, etc., inside a wife's hut was also important. The hut was by custom divided (not by a wall, but by understanding) into two halves. The left-hand side as you enter the hut was called the *lower* side (*emwalo*); the right-hand side was called the *upper* side (*emukulu*). The lower side had the sleeping area of the parents, and therefore married children were not allowed to step that way under any circumstances. It also had the hearth for warming or for cooking. The upper side is where the rest of the furniture (pots, etc.) was kept. Married sons and daughters could sit that way provided the door was left wide open, even if it was night.

3. WALLED VILLAGES

There were walled villages in many parts of Buluyia. That is, instead of fencing the home with euphorbia or with thorns, a wall of clay was built

LUYIA HOME OF A MAN WITH SEVEN WIVES AND FOUR ADULT SONS

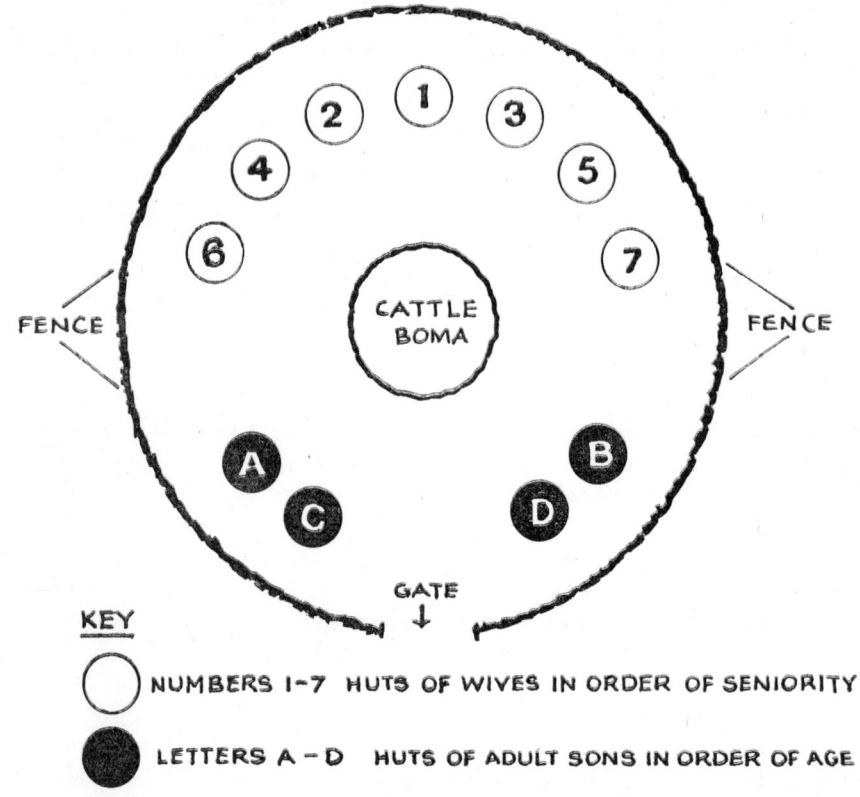

KEY

○ NUMBERS 1–7 HUTS OF WIVES IN ORDER OF SENIORITY

● LETTERS A–D HUTS OF ADULT SONS IN ORDER OF AGE

round the huts. Outside the wall usually ran a ditch (*olukoba*) all round The walled villages were a protection against night raids by the Teso, or the Abakwabi (Masai), who were generally known as Abaseebe.

Walled villages were commonest in Bukusu (e.g. Lumboka and Chetambe's), Bukhayo, Samia, and Bunyala in Busia District, and in Wanga.

One of the early Europeans to enter Buluyia, a German called Carl Peters, described the walled village of Chief Sakwa in Wanga Mukulu as follows:

'A wide ditch surrounds the walls of the palace, over which a dam leads to the gate. On entering the enclosure the stranger first comes upon a great open space, surrounded by the houses of the war garrison of the palace. From thence he comes to a second great space, which is surrounded, in a wide circle, by the many houses of the Sultan. All these houses are full of hundreds of women, in whose midst he himself dwells.'

Chapter 15

Obtaining Food and Tools

1. DISTRIBUTION OF LAND IN OLD DAYS

In the old days land in Buluyia belonged to the clan. Each family belonging to the clan had its own plots as its share of this land. A person could give a plot of land to a member of another clan to cultivate for a time, but the plot could not be bought and it always remained the property of the family in particular and the clan in general. In a similar way, the tribe to which the clan belonged defended the clan's right over its land.

At times when it was necessary to cultivate in one small place, to keep wild animals out, every member of a village or *olukongo* temporarily got a little share of the area and they all cultivated their little temporary plots without consideration of to which clan the land belonged. When the season was over, the land reverted to the rightful owners.

When a man died, his land was handed down either to his eldest son or divided between all the sons, according to custom. Usually, however, a man, while he was still alive, gave plots to each of his married sons. The remaining plots would then go to the unmarried sons.

2. GETTING FOOD FROM THE LAND AND THE ANIMALS

The Abaluyia grew the following crops: sorghum, finger millet, simsim, a variety of nuts, especially *tsimbande*, a variety of peas, especially *tsing'oli*, pumpkins, sweet potatoes, bananas, and in the Mt. Elgon area, yams.

From their domestic animals they got meat and milk and, of course, butter and ghee. They also got meat from the wild animals they killed.

They caught termites and locusts and made rare food out of them. They also killed birds and collected fruits and wild vegetables.

Where fish was available, it was used.

3. DIVISION OF LABOUR

This was treated in detail in Chapter 2 and should be revised in reference to that chapter.

4. BLACKSMITHS

These were very special people and they belonged to particular families and clans only. The most outstanding clan known for its blacksmithing practices was Abang'aale. Branches of this clan are found in most places in Buluyia. In Samia they are known as Abang'aale. In Bunyore they are called Abamang'ali. In most other places they are called Abang'ali. Wherever they were found their trade was making iron tools: hoes, axes, knives of all shapes, spears, arrow-heads, bangles, and other iron implements.

There were, of course, other clans which practised blacksmithing, but they were not so widespread as the Abamang'ali.

The iron ore (*oburale*) was found in certain hills, e.g. the Samia Hills. It was taken into the smithy (*lirumbi*) where it was smelted and then shaped by using a forked bellows.

Iron tools were rare and much sought after. Some of them were used as a means of exchange, as there was no money then.

The iron trade was handed down from father to son.

5. HANDCRAFTS, POTTERY AND BASKETRY

Other families specialized in handcrafts and the making of pots and baskets.

Among the handcrafts were musical instruments like drums and harps; also stools, wooden hoe handles, wooden vessels (e.g. *eshinu*), and so on.

The various types of pots and baskets were mentioned in an earlier chapter and should be revised. They also made fishing traps, ropes and mats.

6. FARMING TODAY

Great changes have taken place. Instead of the little hoe, it is now possible to use a plough or a tractor. Large areas can be cultivated, and many people now realize that it is easier to farm a large continuous stretch of land than to cultivate isolated plots as in the old days.

New crops have been introduced into Buluyia; for instance, maize, groundnuts, cotton, sugar cane, cassava, and some coffee. These are grown mainly for cash.

7. SALT

In the old days salt was made by burning grass taken from a swamp. The ashes were passed through water. The resulting liquid was boiled into a hard cake which was wrapped in dry banana leaves for storing or export.

Chapter 16

Sending Messages

1. THE OLD METHOD

In the old days there were no proper roads and no communications as we know them today. It was difficult to send news from one place to another distant place.

When the Baluyia wanted to send a message about a well-understood happening, they used drums or horns. If there was a plan to start a great tribal festival, they used drums and horns to announce it. If a great person died, they used them too. They also used them at weddings, at the 'crowning of a new chief, the approach of an enemy, and the declaration of war, or' its end.

In cases of a war or the approach of enemies, as soon as the first drums and horns were heard, they were repeated in every *olukongo*, and thus the message was relayed on.

Sometimes weeping aloud, as in the case of a funeral, or shouting, as in the case of a fleeing thief, was used to spread the message.

People also spread news through greeting by asking, '*Akasungwa?*' Also, a messenger could be sent to deliver special news verbally.

2. SENDING MESSAGES TODAY

It is much easier to send a message nowadays. You can post a letter or send a telegram. You can speak to a person on the telephone. For general news, you can read the newspaper or listen to the radio or watch television.

Travelling has also become much quicker with bicycles, motor vehicles, trains, and even aeroplanes.

Chapter 17

Some Customs of the Neighbouring Tribes

1. THE TESO

The Teso are Nilotic and speak a completely different language from Luluyia. Their customs are also different. For instance, they remove two lower teeth instead of four and six. They used to be hostile to strangers, and the Baluyia say that no one could pass through Teso country without being killed. The Abakhayo have many things in common with the Teso because they live so close together. The Baluyia of the west have borrowed a Teso word for greeting—it is '*yoga*'. The Teso live in the same region as the Baluyia, in Busia District.

2. THE LUO

The Luo are Nilotic and also speak a different language from Luluyia. Many of their customs of birth, initiation and death have been copied by the western Abaluyia: for instance, naming. The Luos name their children according to the time of day or of the year when they are born, or according to the circumstances in which they are born.

Boy	*Girl*	*Meaning*
Otieno	Atieno	Born at night
Okinyi	Akinyi	Born early in the morning
Okumu	Akumu	Born after twins
Odoyo	Adoyo	Born during weeding

and so on. The Baluyia of the west have adopted all of these names.

Here are some typical Luyia names which are not borrowed:

Boy	*Girl*	*Meaning*
Wafula	Nafula	Born during rain
Wasike	Nasike	Born during locusts
Wabwire	Nabwire	Born at night
Wanjala	Nanjala	Born during a famine
Wekesa	Nekesa	Born during the harvest

and so on. These names are not often found among the Baluyia of the east.

Some Customs of the Neighbouring Tribes

Names for twins are regular too in Buluyia. The first to come is called Balongo and the other Mukhwana. In western Buluyia they are called Apiyo and Adongo, respectively. Again there is Luo influence in this.

Removing teeth: The Luos remove six teeth of the lower jaw at puberty. The western Baluyia also remove six due to Luo influence. But the Baluyia of the east remove four, if at all.

Tattooing: Luo women used to tattoo their abdomens and foreheads as well as the back. Some Baluyia also did this.

3. THE ELKONY AND THE NANDI

They are Nilo-Hamitic and of the same stock (Kalenjin). Their customs include:

Circumcision: They circumcise all boys and in some areas they circumcise girls too.

Boring ears: They used to bore their ears and let them hang.

The Elkony live in Western Province; the Nandi are found in the Rift Valley Province. They are related to the Nyang'ori, who are also in the Rift Valley Province, but were formerly in Buluyia.

4. UASIN GISHU MASAI

They used to be called Abakwabi, but nowadays they are generally referred to as Abaseebe. It seems that the strange type of secret cult in Buluyia called *emiseebe* originates from these people. For the Abaluyia who become *Abaseebe* tend to behave like the ancient Masai, and speak a strange dialect. The Masai are Nilo-Hamitic. They too circumcise their young people. They call themselves Sabaot.

5. THE KISII

They originally came from the same ancestor as the Abalogoli, and so they are really Luyia in origin. They have clans similar to those of Abaluyia, and their legends are also almost identical with those of Buluyia. The Kisii are found in the Nyanza Province. They call themselves Gusii.

6. THE SUBA

These are also related to the Kisii and the Maragoli. They live on the islands of Rusinga and Mfwang'ano. They are Bantu and in their families they still speak the Bantu language. But because they live close to the Luo, they have adopted Luo customs and also the Luo language.

Note: Some Baluyia circumcise, some do not. Generally speaking, the western ones do not circumcise, while the eastern ones do. In this case the western ones implies all the Baluyia in Busia District.

Chapter 18
The Recent History of Buluyia

1. THE DEVELOPMENT OF ADMINISTRATION
   The British administration was established in Buluyia in 1894. The whole of the area was then in Uganda. A sub-station was established at Mumias in 1894 and Mr. Spire was in charge. Mr. C. W. Hobley became the first Provincial Commissioner of the whole of Nyanza in 1895. With the help of Mumia all the tribes of the area were brought under British rule by Hobley, whom the Baluyia called '*Obilo*'. The capital which was at Mumias was later moved to Kisumu.

   At first Wanga chiefs were sent to rule various areas. But later they were replaced by local chiefs. Mumia himself became paramount chief in 1909 and retired from it in 1926.

   At first Buluyia was one district called North Kavirondo. Maragoli, part of Tiriki, and Bunyore were in the Luo district of Central Nyanza. Later Maragoli and Bunyore were returned to North Kavirondo, but western Bunyala and Samia were removed to Central Nyanza.

   In 1952 Mr. W. W. W. Awori was the first Muluyia to enter the Legislative Council.

   In 1956 the Luyia district was divided into two: North Nyanza and Elgon Nyanza. Mr. P. Nabwana was the first president of an African District Council in Kenya—in Elgon Nyanza.

   In 1963 Samia and Bunyala were removed from Central Nyanza and placed in the new Busia District. At the same time the locations of Marach, Bukhayo and Teso were removed from Elgon Nyanza and also placed in the Busia District. As a result, there are now three districts in the Western Province: Kakamega, Bungoma and Busia.

2. PROGRESS IN MISSIONARY WORK
   The chief missionary bodies which still carry out their activities in Buluyia are: the Church Missionary Society (CMS); the Friends African Mission (FAM); the Catholic Mill Hill Mission (MHM); the Pentecostal Assemblies of East Africa (PAEA); the Church of God (COG); and the Salvation Army.

The CMS arrived around 1906 and opened a school in Maseno as early as 1908. Later they started a hospital there. Another mission school was opened at Butere (1927).

The Mill Hill Mission entered Kenya from Uganda. The priests made regular visits to Buluyia from as early as 1902, and opened a mission station at Mumias in 1904. Many other missions followed: Mukumu in 1906; Eregi in 1912; Nangina in 1927; Kibabii in 1931; Butula in 1937; Port Victoria in 1938. They have also opened many more missions since.

The Church of God started at Kima between 1905 and 1906. Then Ingotse (1925) in Butsotso, and Mwihila (1938) was started in Kisa.

The Friends African Missionaries arrived in Kenya in 1902 and opened a mission at Kaimosi in Tiriki in the same year. They also started a mission in Isukha at Lirhanda and another at Vihiga (1906). Later they extended their activities to other areas of Buluyia: Lugulu in Bukusu (1914) and Malaba in Kabras (1918). At Kaimosi they opened a hospital.

The Salvation Army opened their first mission in Buluyia in 1936, at Malakisi. The Pentecostal Assemblies had opened a mission at Nyang'ori in 1924. The two missions have since spread to other places.

Some Africans started their own breakaway Christian sects. *Dini ya Roho* was founded by Alfayo Mango and Labi Obonyo in 1934. There were serious disturbances between the Baluyia and Luos in Musanda (Uholo) as a result.

Another religious sect which brought trouble was the *Dini ya Misambwa* founded by Elijah Masinde in 1948. The religion was later proscribed by the Kenya government, but has been permitted to function again.

There are other religious sects too, such as the *African Israeli*.

3. PROGRESS IN EDUCATION

At first all education was carried out by the missionary bodies. They were called voluntary bodies and later (1925) they were given financial grants-in-aid by government to help them run the schools.

In 1931 Kakamega Government Secondary School was started to supplement the missionary schools such as Maseno and Butere (CMS), St. Mary's Yala (MHM), Kaimosi (FAM), and Kima (COG).

The District Education Board of North Nyanza was set up in 1934, to supervise primary education.

At first great stress was laid on boys' education, because African parents were not keen on giving their daughters a school education. Later some girls' schools were opened by the missions. These included: Mukumu Girls' School (MHM); Butere Girls' School (CMS); and a few others.

4. DEVELOPMENT OF AGRICULTURE

The first agricultural school was opened at Bukura in Butsotso location in 1923. It began to train agricultural instructors to advise farmers who were being encouraged to plant new crops such as maize, groundnuts, cotton and so on. Free seed was at first issued by the government.

The veterinary school at Sang'aalo was opened in 1924.

5. ECONOMIC DEVELOPMENT

At first the Baluyia had little value for the money of the white man. Later when shopping centres began to spread in Buluyia and useful articles were sold, this idea changed. The Baluyia began to buy things like salt, *sufurias*, and clothes. Moreover the government wanted everyone to pay tax. This forced many Baluyia to seek employment on European farms and other places.

Indians opened a trading centre at Mumias in 1902, and at Kakamega in 1903. Later other trading centres were opened at: Lunyelele in Maragoli, Kimilili in Bukusu, Butere in Marama, Luanda in Bunyore, Nambale in Bukhayo, Sio Port in Samia, and several other places.

Gold mines were started in Kakamega in 1932, but they did not last long; however, they taught the Baluyia to value money, and many more than before now went to seek employment.

Today many Baluyia have shops or other businesses of their own or are large farmers.

6. MEDICAL SERVICES

A temporary hospital was built at Mumias in 1910. It was followed by the introduction of mobile dispensaries, which travelled all over the district. Finally a permanent government hospital was built at Kakamega in 1922. Some missions also opened hospitals.

7. TO SUM UP

This then is a brief story of how the people of Buluyia lived from the early times to modern times. It is intended only to give a general idea about how our ancestors lived and felt during that period. In these fast-changing times it is easy for an African to forget, ignore or even despise the kind of life and the culture that gave birth to him. This is not right. Although we cannot live as our ancestors lived, we ought at least to understand why they lived like that and why things have changed since then. We must never give the impression that their way of life was unhappy, their customs and traditions silly, and their dances and songs evil. On the contrary, the children ought to realize that there were many good things in the culture of our ancestors which we ought to preserve, while at the same time knowing that some others were useful at that time but would be out of date in our time.

The important thing is that the children should learn about our past not to despise but to appreciate, not to copy simply, but to profit by the knowledge, not to contrast, but to compare. An African child needs an African culture to give him a sense of belonging, a sense of pride in his worth and a sense of confidence in today's international world. This does not mean that he should discard everything modern and go back to what was once Africa; it means making the best use of both what was good in the old, and what is good in the new. The teacher of history in the primary school has, therefore, a duty to make the children understand and appreciate the best ideals of their ancestors and to help them relate this to the best ideals of modern society.

8. KENYA TODAY

Another point that should be put across to the children is that Buluyia is now part of the Kenya nation. It so happens that the first booklet of this kind to come out is on the Baluyia, but other booklets on other tribes will be written sooner or later; and no efforts should be spared to make the Baluyia children understand that other tribes are like us, and we are now all members of one nation.

FUNDERBURG LIBRARY
MANCHESTER COLLEGE

916.762
Os 5l